GREAT LIVES OBSERVED

Gerald Emanuel Stearn, *General Editor*

EACH VOLUME IN THE SERIES VIEWS THE CHARACTER AND
ACHIEVEMENT OF A GREAT WORLD FIGURE IN THREE PER-
SPECTIVES—THROUGH HIS OWN WORDS, THROUGH THE OPIN-
IONS OF HIS CONTEMPORARIES, AND THROUGH RETROSPEC-
TIVE JUDGMENTS—THUS COMBINING THE INTIMACY OF AUTO-
BIOGRAPHY, THE IMMEDIACY OF EYEWITNESS OBSERVATION,
AND THE OBJECTIVITY OF MODERN SCHOLARSHIP.

MORTON BORDEN, *the editor of this volume in the Great Lives
Observed series, is Professor of History at the University of
California, Santa Barbara. His previous works include* The
Federalism of James A. Bayard, America's Ten Greatest Presi-
dents, The Antifederalist Papers, Parties and Politics in the
Early Republic, *as well as numerous articles and book reviews
in historical journals.*

GREAT LIVES OBSERVED

GEORGE
WASHINGTON

Edited by MORTON BORDEN

*Who believes that Washington could write as good a book
or report as Jefferson, or make as able a speech as Hamilton?
Who is there that believes that Cromwell would have
made as good a judge as Lord Hale? No, sir; these learned
and accomplishd men find their proper place under
those who are fitted to command, and to command them
among the rest. Such a man as Washington will say to a
Jefferson, do you become my Secretary of State; to Hamilton,
do you take charge of my purse, or that of the nation,
which is the same thing; and to Knox, do you be master
of the horse. All history shows this; but great logicians
and great scholars are for that very reason unfit to be rulers.*

—JOHN RANDOLPH

A SPECTRUM BOOK

PRENTICE-HALL, INC., ENGLEWOOD CLIFFS, N.J.

The quotation on the title page is from a speech before Congress given February 1, 1828, and quoted in
John Randolph of Roanoke, by Russell Kirk (Chicago,
1964).

For Lucy and Kate, ardent admirers of George Washington

Copyright © 1969 by PRENTICE-HALL, INC.
Englewood Cliffs, New Jersey.

A SPECTRUM BOOK

Current printing (last number):

10 9 8 7 6 5 4 3 2 1

C–13–945493–4

P–13–945485–3

Library of Congress Catalog Card Number: 74–90974

Printed in the United States of America

PRENTICE-HALL INTERNATIONAL INC. (*London*)
PRENTICE-HALL OF AUSTRALIA, PTY. LTD. (*Sydney*)
PRENTICE-HALL OF CANADA, LTD. (*Toronto*)
PRENTICE-HALL OF INDIA PRIVATE LIMITED (*New Delhi*)
PRENTICE-HALL OF JAPAN, INC. (*Tokyo*)

Contents

Fifty contemporary documents commenting on George Washington, from the Indian Half-King's peevish account in 1754 to Thomas Jefferson's balanced summary in 1814.

PART THREE
WASHINGTON IN HISTORY

Introduction

"Did any body ever see Washington nude?" asked Nathaniel Hawthorne in 1858. "It is inconceivable. He had no nakedness, but I imagine he was born with his clothes on, and his hair powdered, and made a stately bow on his first appearance in the world." Hawthorne, of course, was poking fun at the image rather than the man, but to the American public in the nineteenth century the two were indistinguishable: any criticism of Washington bordered on blasphemy. If some philosophically inclined individuals refused to join in the deification of Washington, insisting that men, while good enough, are far more complex and fascinating than mere divinities, they were in a distinct minority.

The pietistic biographies of the nineteenth century obscured the figure of Washington; so did the "debunking" studies of the 1920's, which went to the opposite extreme. If the former tried to elevate Washington to superhuman status by relentlessly describing his wisdom and goodness, the latter tried to deconsecrate Washington by citing examples of what the authors took to be his envy, greed, shallowness, and hypocrisy. It is difficult to say which of the genres constituted the greater perversion. Certainly neither is balanced. To recognize only his virtues is to ignore the rich contradictions inherent in the human personality; to recognize only his liabilities is to ignore the reasons for his greatness.

Why, then, was Washington great? In what did he excel? By common consent his intellectual talents were limited. He knew little of science or philosophy or political theory. He had no sparkling wit, no quick perceptions, no clever insights to offer. Scholars interested in conceptual originality, in mental ferment, in the clash of ideas, must turn elsewhere. Indeed, sophisticated twentieth-century historians seem to be more intrigued by the diffusion of the Washington legend than by the man himself. His military talents have been endlessly debated, but surely America has produced abler strategists and tacticians. His presidential talents have received mixed ratings. One might argue that between 1789 and 1797 Washington left unresolved as many problems as he solved, and probably created a few new ones. The proclamation of neutrality and Jay's treaty may have appeased the British, but they aggravated American relations with France. The suppression of the Whiskey Rebellion served to spur the very growth of party spirit which Washington abhorred. After eight years in office, Jefferson wrote, Washington "is fortunate to get off just as the bubble is bursting, leaving others to hold the bag."

It should be no surprise, then, that an appreciation of Washington's greatness must inevitably turn upon the point of character, not talent. Were this not so, he would be simply another Virginia planter, blooded in the colonial wars, who by a lucky turn of events defeated the British and was elevated by an adoring public to the position of chief magistrate. But his character *was* superior, a fact which his contemporaries recognized, and in which all commentators from John Marshall to Douglas S. Freeman have concurred.

Foremost was his remarkable dedication to American independence. When officers quarreled over rank and honors; when state governments were tardy and remiss in supplying food, clothing, and troop quotas; when men deserted; when currency became hopelessly inflated; when French naval support seemed an infinity away—Washington, though subject to occasional doubts and despair—persevered in the revolutionary cause. Joined to perseverance was his fundamentally realistic approach to problems. He knew at the outset of the war that Britain possessed greater manpower and mobility, and that he must adhere to an enforced defensive. Sometimes he moved so slowly, so cautiously, that his leadership was questioned and his competence doubted. But the ultimate conquest of the British army was due to Washington's prolonged reluctance to risk a major battle at unequal odds. Yorktown was the result of six years of patience and fortitude.

Washington's eminently practical turn of mind gave to the American revolution substance and actuality. It was evident when, on one hand, he exhorted his troops to superior efforts in a patriotic cause against mercenary hirelings; and, on the other, when he warned Congress that patriotism was not an enduring incentive, that pay and promotion were more vital in moving armies to fight. It was evident when, on one hand, he welcomed the French as brothers in arms, as an ally who had given "repeated assurances and proofs of friendship"; and, on the other, when he warned Congress in 1778 to beware of an extension of French military influence in the new world, for she "would, it is much to be apprehended, have it in her power to give law to these states." This was the voice neither of duplicity nor hypocrisy, but of hard-headed reason and common sense.

Though practical, Washington's character was not simple. He attempted to maintain the highest standards of personal and professional integrity. Yet in one glaring instance, Washington was capable of ordering a minister to obtain military information from two captured spies under the guise of offering them spiritual consolation. He detested the institution of slavery. Yet Washington sold slaves, deplored Quaker attempts at manumission, and was shocked when slaves revolted. He took pride in remaining impervious to public criticism. Yet Washington was really inordinately conscious of and sensitive to the opinion of his peers. Concern for his country and concern for his reputation seem to intermingle in Washington's thoughts.

Complex he was: a revolutionary leader of essentially conservative qualities, a military man deeply committed to republicanism, a provincial Virginian whose revolutionary experience matured his continental perspectives. "We are placed among the nations of the earth, and have a character to establish," Washington noted at the close of the war. "But how we shall acquit ourselves time will discover." Would the United States repeat the tragic European cycle of wars, poverty, despotism, and corruption? Or would the United States become a country of peace and liberty, unified and prosperous? No one could doubt the potential. Independence had been gained and freedom proclaimed. The land was rich. The West—a *"second land of promise"* Washington called it— beckoned to settlers. Neither could one doubt the risks. Cultural cleavages, sectional jealousies, economic rivalries, all had to be surmounted. Much depended upon the emerging American character. Washington's most significant contribution was to set an example of what that character should be.

The example was not always praised. In the delicate balance which democracies must maintain between liberty and order, Washington, under the strain of party divisions in the 1790's, overstressed order. But it was order tempered with justice. He indulged himself in the accoutrements of aristocracy—a handsome coach and livery and powdered lackeys—which Republicans worried would develop into monarchical precedents. But Washington's unquestioned devotion to republicanism made this unlikely. His approval of Alexander Hamilton's financial plans and constitutional interpretations led some contemporaries and later scholars to conclude that he was manipulated by the Secretary of the Treasury. To be sure, Hamilton was unusually persuasive, and Washington appreciated his abilities. But both as general and as president—although it was his custom to seek the advice of others—Washington was always his own man. Emotionally he had much more in common with his fellow Virginians, Thomas Jefferson and James Madison: a love of that land and the plantation way of life. By conviction, however, he was a nationalist, and his agreement with Hamilton was logically consistent with all his previous expressions.

Even Washington's political opponents, while criticizing him for what he did, came in time to praise him for what he was: the symbol of the best America had to offer. Not infallible. Certainly not a saint. But a man of the finest motivations, aware of his limitations, as indispensable as any leader ever was or could be, who made possible the achievement of independence and the success of federal union.

Chronology of the
Life of George Washington

1732   Born February 22 (February 11, old style) on a plantation by Pope's Creek, Westmoreland County, Virginia.

1743   Death of Washington's father.

1748   Goes to live with brother Lawrence at Mount Vernon; appointed assistant surveyor for Lord Fairfax in March.

1749   Appointed official surveyor for Culpeper County.

1751   Voyage to Barbados; attack of smallpox.

1752   Joins Masonic order; appointed a Major in the Virginia militia.

1753   Sent by Governor Dinwiddie to deliver an ultimatum to the French in the Ohio valley.

1754   Appointed Lieutenant Colonel of Virginia militia. Resigns commission in October.

1755   Appointed aide-de-camp to General Braddock in May; Colonel of Virginia troops in August.

1758   Resigns military commission. Wins first election as Burgess for Frederick County, receiving 310 votes of 794 cast.

1759   Married to Mrs. Martha Dandridge Custis on January 6.

1761   Re-elected Burgess.

1762   Vestryman, Truro Parish, Fairfax County.

1763   Warden of Pohick church, Truro Parish.

1765   Elected Burgess for Fairfax County.

1768   Re-elected Burgess.

1769   Re-elected Burgess. Helps organize a boycott of British goods.

1770   Justice of the peace, Fairfax County. Journeys to western Pennsylvania and Ohio.

1771   Re-elected Burgess.

1773   Journey to New York City.

1774   Re-elected Burgess. Attends Virginia Provincial Convention at Williamsburg in August, and is appointed one of seven Virginia delegates to the first Continental Congress in Philadelphia.

1775   Elected to second Continental Congress in March; named Commander in Chief of American forces in June; takes command at Cambridge in July.

1776	Occupies Boston; battles at Long Island, White Plains, and Trenton.
1777	Battles at Princeton, Brandywine, and Germantown. Winter headquarters at Valley Forge.
1778	Battle at Monmouth. Winter headquarters at Middlebrook.
1781	Accepts surrender of Cornwallis at Yorktown.
1783	Named President of the Society of the Cincinnati. Resigns military commission.
1784	Attends conference concerning navigation of Potomac river.
1785	President of Potomac company.
1787	Member of the Virginia delegation to the Constitutional Convention in Philadelphia. Named President of the Convention.
1788	Elected Chancellor of William and Mary College.
1789	Elected President of the United States. Death of Washington's mother. Tours New England in October and November.
1790	Visits Rhode Island.
1791	Tours Southern states in April and June.
1792	Re-elected President of the United States.
1797	Retires and returns to Mount Vernon.
1798	Appointed Lieutenant General and Commander in Chief of the American armies.
1799	Dies at Mount Vernon on December 14.
1802	Death of Martha Washington.

PART ONE

WASHINGTON LOOKS AT THE WORLD[1]

1

Frontier Fighter and Virginia Planter, 1753–1774

"*I heard the bullets whistle,*" *Washington wrote in 1754, "and, believe me, there is something charming in the sound." He was then twenty-two, aspired to military fame, and displayed an unbecoming aggressiveness for promotion and recognition. Soon thereafter Washington settled contentedly into the life style of a rich Virginia planter. By the summer of 1775, when he accepted the post of Commander in Chief of the revolutionary forces, Washington was a military man with a civilian heart. He sought no personal glory. He despised war. He wished for nothing more than to remain at Mount Vernon.*

Again, in 1789, when the nation unanimously called upon Washington to serve as its first President, his sense of public duty overcame his marked reluctance to leave the quiet pleasures of private life. Now America required not military direction, but order and stability. "If the President can be preserved a few years till habits of authority and obedience can be established generally," Jefferson noted in 1790, "we have nothing to fear." Despite the political buffeting he received, Washington agreed to serve not one, but two terms of office, thus giving the new nation what above all else it needed: time.

[1] The selected excerpts of Washington's letters, diaries, and military orders are taken from John C. Fitzpatrick, ed., *The Writings of George Washington* (Washington, D.C., 1931–1944), 39 volumes. Some spelling, punctuation, and grammatical changes have been made for better comprehension.

JOURNEY TO THE FRENCH COMMANDANT

December 23, 1753

Just after we had passed a place called the Murdering-Town . . . we fell in with a party of French Indians, who had lain in wait for us. One of them fired at Mr. Gist or me, not 15 steps off, but fortunately missed. We took this fellow into custody, and kept him till about 9 o'clock at night; then let him go, and walked all the remaining part of the night without making any stop that we might get the start so far as to be out of the reach of their pursuit the next day, since we were well assured they would follow our track as soon as it was light. The next day we continued travelling till quite dark, and got to the river. . . . There was no way for getting over but on a raft, which we set about with but one poor hatchet, and finished just after sun-setting. This was a whole day's work. Then set off; but before we were half way over, we were jammed in the ice, in such a manner that we expected every moment our raft to sink, and ourselves to perish. I put out my setting pole to try to stop the raft, that the ice might pass by, when the rapidity of the stream threw it with so much violence against the pole, that it jerked me out into ten feet water. But I fortunately saved myself by catching hold of one of the raft logs. Notwithstanding all our efforts we could not get the raft to either shore; but were obliged, as we were near an island, to quit our raft and make to it.

The cold was so extremely severe, that Mr. Gist had all his fingers, and some of his toes frozen; but the water was shut up so hard, that we found no difficulty in getting off the island, on the ice, in the morning, and went to Mr. Frazier's.

TO RICHARD CORBIN

Alexandria, March, 1754

In a conversation with you at Green Spring, you gave me some room to hope for a commission above that of major, and to be ranked among the chief officers of this expedition. The command of the whole forces is what I neither look for, expect, nor desire; for I must be impartial enough to confess, it is a charge too great for my youth and inexperience to be entrusted with. Knowing this, I have too sincere a love for my country, to undertake that which may tend to the prejudice of it. But if I could entertain hopes that you thought me worthy of the post of lieutenant-colonel, and would favor me so far as to mention it at the appointment of officers, I could not but entertain a true sense of the kindness.

TO JOHN AUGUSTINE WASHINGTON

Great Meadow, May 31, 1754

Three days ago we had an engagement with the French, that is, a party of our men with one of theirs. Most of our men were out upon other detachments, so that I had scarcely 40 men remaining under my command, and about 10 or 12 Indians; nevertheless we obtained a most signal victory. The battle lasted about 10 or 15 minutes, with sharp firing on both sides, till the French gave ground and ran, but to no great purpose. There were 12 killed of the French, among whom was Mons. de Jumonville, their commander, and 21 taken prisoners. . . .

P.S. I fortunately escaped without any wound, for the right wing, where I stood, was exposed to and received all the enemy's fire. . . . I heard the bullets whistle, and, believe me, there is something charming in the sound.

TO JOHN AUGUSTINE WASHINGTON

Fort Cumberland, May 14, 1755

The General has appointed me one of his aids de camps, in which character I shall serve this campaign, agreeably enough, as I am thereby freed from all commands but his, and give orders to all, which must be implicitly obeyed.

I have now a good opportunity, and shall not neglect it, of forming an acquaintance, which may be serviceable hereafter, if I can find it worthwhile pushing my fortune in the military way.

TO ROBERT DINWIDDIE

Fort Cumberland, July 18, 1755

When we came to this place, we were attacked (very unexpectedly I must own) by about 300 French and Indians. Our numbers consisted of about 1300 well armed men, chiefly regulars, who were immediately struck with such a deadly panic, that nothing but confusion and disobedience of orders prevailed amongst them. The Officers in general behaved with incomparable bravery, for which they greatly suffered, there being near 60 killed and wounded. A large proportion, out of the number we had! The Virginian Companies behaved like men and died like soldiers; for I believe out of the 3 companys that were there that day, scarce 30 were left alive. . . . The dastardly behavior of the English soldiers exposed all those who were inclined to do their duty to almost certain death; and at length, despite every effort to the contrary, broke and ran as sheep before the hounds, leaving the Artillery, Ammunition, Provisions, and every individual thing we had with us a prey to the enemy; and when we endeavored to rally them in hopes of regaining our invaluable loss, it was with as much success as if we had attempted to have stopped the wild bears of the mountains. The General [Braddock] was wounded behind in the shoulder, and into the breast, of which he died three days after. . . . I luckily escaped without a wound though I had four bullets through my coat and two horses shot under me.

TO JOHN AUGUSTINE WASHINGTON

Mount Vernon, August 2, 1755

I was employed to go a journey in the Winter . . . and what did I get by it? My expenses borne! I then was appointed with trifling pay to conduct a handful of men to the Ohio. What did I get by this? Why, after putting myself to a considerable expence in equipping and providing necessarys for the campaign I went out, was soundly beaten, lost them all—came in, and had my Commission taken from me or, in other words, my Commission reduced, under pretence of an order from home. I then went out a volunteer with General Braddock and lost all my horses and many other things, but this being a voluntary act, I should not have mentioned it, was it not to show that I have been upon the losing order ever since I entered the service, which is now near two years. So that I think I can't be blamed should I, if I leave my family again, endeavor to do it upon such terms as to . . . gain by it.

TO ENSIGN DENNIS MCCARTHY

Fredericksburg, November 22, 1755

I am very sorry you have given me occasion to complain of your conduct in recruiting; and to tell you, that the methods and unjustifiable means you have practised, are very unacceptable, and have been of infinite prejudice to the Service. Of this I am informed by many gentlemen, as well as by all the Officers who were ordered to recruit in these parts; and am further assured, that it is next to an impossibility to get a man where you have been; such terror have you occasioned by forcibly taking, confining and torturing those who would not voluntarily enlist. These proceedings not only cast a slur upon your own character, but reflect dishonor upon mine; as giving room to conjecture, that they have my concurrence for their source.

TO CAPTAIN JOHN ASHBY

Winchester, December 28, 1755

I am very much surprised to hear the great irregularities which were allowed of in your camp. The rum, although sold by Joseph Coombs, I am credibly informed, is your property. There are continual complaints to me of the misbehavior of your wife, who I am told sows sedition among the men, and is chief of every mutiny. If she is not immediately sent from the camp, or I hear any more complaints of such irregular behavior upon my arrival there, I shall take care to drive her out myself, and suspend you.

TO ROBERT DINWIDDIE

Winchester, April 27, 1756

Desolation and murder still increase, and no prospects of relief. The Blue Ridge is now our frontier, no men being left in this county, except a few that keep close with a number of women and children in forts, which they have erected for that purpose. . . . We have the greatest reason in life to believe that the number of the enemy is very considerable, as they are spread all over this part of the country; and that their success, and the spoils with which they have enriched themselves, dished up with a good deal of French policy, will encourage the Indians of distant nations to fall upon our inhabitants in greater numbers, and, if possible, with greater rapidity. They enjoy the sweets of a profitable war, and will no doubt improve the success, which ever must attend their arms, without we have Indians to oppose theirs. I would therefore advise, as I often have done, that there should be neither trouble nor expense omitted to bring the few, who are still inclined, into our service, and that, too, with the greatest care and expedition.

SPEECH TO THE TUSCARORAS

Winchester, August 1, 1756

Brothers, You can be no strangers to the many murders and cruelties committed on our countrymen and friends, by that false and faithless people the French, who are constantly endeavoring to corrupt the minds of our friendly Indians; and have stirred up the Shawnees and Delawares, with several other nations to take up the hatchet against us. . . . Many of these Indians have invaded our country, laid waste our lands, plundered our plantations, murdered defenceless women and children, and burnt and destroyed wherever they came; which has enraged our friends the Six Nations, Cherokees, Nottoways, Catawbas, and all our Indian Allies, and prompted them to take up the hatchet in our defence, against these disturbers of the common peace.

I hope, Brothers, you will likewise take up the hatchet against the French and their Indians, as our other friends have done, and send us some of your young men, to protect our frontiers, and go to war with us, against our restless and ambitious foes. And to encourage your brave Warriors, I promise to furnish them with arms, ammunition, clothes, provision, and every necessary for war. And the sooner you send them to our assistance, the greater mark will you give us of your friendship; and the better shall we be enabled to take just revenge of their cruelties.

TO ROBERT DINWIDDIE

Winchester, August 4, 1756

I could by no means bring the Quakers to any terms. They chose rather to be whipped to death than bear arms, or lend us any assistance whatever upon the fort, or any thing of self-defence. Some of their friends have been security for their appearance, when they are called for; and I have released them from the guard-house until I receive further orders from your Honor, which they have agreed to apply for.

SPEECH TO CAPTAIN JOHNNE, CATAWBAS

Winchester, October 28, 1756

We desire you to go to the Cherokees, and tell them the road is now clear and open. We expected them to war last Spring, and love them so well, that our Governor sent some few men to build a fort among them. But we are mighty sorry that they hearken so much to lies French tell, as to break their promise and not come to war, when they might have got a great deal of honor, and killed a great many of the French, whose hearts are false, and rotten as an old stump. If they continue to listen to what the French say much longer they will have great cause to be sorry, as the French have no match-locks, powder and lead but what they got from King George our father before the war began and that will soon be out; when they will get no more, and all French Indians will be starving with cold, and must take to bows and arrows again for want of ammunition.

Tell them we long to shake hands with them.

Let them get their knives and tomahawks sharp. We will go before them, and show them the way to honor, scalps, prisoners, and money enough. We are mighty sorry they stay at home idle, when they should go to war, and become great men, and a terror and dread to their enemies. Tell them they shall have victuals enough, and used very kindly.

TO JOHN ROBINSON

Winchester, December 19, 1756

My strongest representations of matters relative to the peace of the frontiers are disregarded as idle and frivolous; my propositions and measures, as partial and selfish; and all my sincerest endeavors for the service of my country perverted to the worst purposes. My orders are dark, doubtful, and uncertain; to-day approved, to-morrow condemned. Left to act and proceed at hazard, accountable for the consequence, and blamed without the benefit of defence! If you can think my situation capable to excite the smallest degree of envy, or afford the least satisfaction, the truth is yet hid from you, and you entertain notions very different from the reality of the case. However, I am determined to

bear up under all the embarrassments some time longer, in hope
of better regulation on the arrival of Lord Loudoun, to whom
I look for the future fate of Virginia. . . .

TO CAPTAIN WILLIAM LIGHTFOOT

Fort Loudoun, June 26, 1757

You are to maintain strict discipline among your men; and
when you are in garrison, to place sentries at proper places by
day and by night. In your marches and countermarches, you are to
be very circumspect, to keep a few alert woodsmen always advanced
before, and on your flanks; and use every precaution to prevent
surprises as you have to deal with a cunning dexterous enemy.

You are not to indulge your men in idleness, but keep them
constantly on the scout, as the most effectual means of answering
the desirable and expected from you, that of protecting the distressed inhabitants.

TO COLONEL HENRY BOUQUET

Fort Cumberland, July 3, 1758

My men are very bare of clothes (Regimentals I mean), and
I have no prospect of a supply. . . . Were I left to pursue my own
inclinations I would not only order the men to adopt the Indian
dress, but cause the officers to do it also, and be the first to
set the example myself. Nothing but the uncertainty of its taking
with the General causes me to hesitate a moment at leaving my
Regimentals at this place, and proceeding as light as any Indian
in the woods. 'Tis an unbecoming dress, I confess, for an officer;
but convenience rather than show, I think should be consulted.

TO MRS. MARTHA CUSTIS

Fort Cumberland, July 20, 1758

We have begun our march for the Ohio. A courier is starting
for Williamsburg, and I embrace the opportunity to send a few
words to one whose life is now inseparable from mine. Since that
happy hour when we made our pledges to each other, my thoughts
have been continually going to you as another self. That an all-
powerful Providence may keep us both in safety is the prayer
of your ever faithful and affectionate friend.

TO RICHARD WASHINGTON

Mount Vernon, May 7, 1759

'Till I hear from you, I have nothing worth mentioning. I have quit a military life; and shortly shall be fixed at this place with an agreeable partner, and then shall be able to conduct my own business with more punctuality than heretofore as it will pass under my own immediate inspection; a thing impracticable while I discharged my duty in the public service of the country.

DIARY

1760

Friday, February 15th. Went to a ball at Alexandria, where music and dancing was the chief entertainment. However in a convenient room detached for the purpose abounded great plenty of bread and butter, some biscuits, with tea and coffee, which the drinkers of could not distinguish from hot water sweetened.

TO ROBERT CARY & COMPANY

Williamsburg, April 3, 1761

I would not have you be hasty in selling this or any of the tobacco I may ship you this year unless a very good market presents itself, for confident I am that the small quantity of tobacco made last year must command a very good price when the fact once becomes well ascertained.

TO ROBERT CARY & COMPANY

Mount Vernon, June 20, 1762

We have had one of the most severe droughts in these parts that ever was known and without a speedy interposition of Providence (in sending us moderate and refreshing rains to mollify and soften the earth) we shall not make one ounce of tobacco this year. Our plants in spite of all our efforts to the contrary are just destroyed, and our grain is absolutely perishing. How it may be in other parts of the country I can not positively say, yet I have heard much complaining.

TO CHARLES LAWRENCE

Williamsburg, April 26, 1763

Be pleased to send me a genteel suit of clothes made of superfine broad cloth handsomely chosen. I should have inclosed you my measure, but in a general way they are so badly taken here that I am convinced it would be of very little service. I would have you therefore take measure of a gentleman who wears well made clothes of the following size: to wit, 6 feet high and proportionably made; if anything rather slender than thick for a person of that height, with pretty long arms and thighs. You will take care to make the breeches longer than those you sent me last.

TO BURWELL BASSETT

Mount Vernon, July 5, 1763

Our wheat in this part of the country is in a great measure destroyed by the rust, and other defect in the ear; and our crops of Indian corn and tobacco in a manner lost in weeds and grass, occasioned by continual excessive rains, that has not only forced these out in very uncommon abundance, but prevented all sorts of tillage where our lands lay flat.

TO RICHARD WASHINGTON

Mount Vernon, September 27, 1763

In the event of your ever visiting America, I am in hopes you will not think a little time ill spent in a small tour to Virginia. We have few things here striking to European travellers (except an abundant woods); but a little variety, a welcome reception among a few friends, and the open and prevalent hospitality of the country in general, might perhaps prove agreeable for a while; and I must be permitted to add, that I shall think myself very happy in seeing you at Mt. Vernon where you might depend upon finding the most cordial entertainment.

TO FRANCIS DANDRIDGE

Mount Vernon, September 20, 1765

The Stamp Act imposed on the colonies by the Parliament of Great Britain engrosses the conversation of the speculative part of the colonists, who look upon this unconstitutional method of taxation as a direful attack upon their liberties, and loudly exclaim against the violation. What may be the result of this and some other (I think I may add) ill judged measures, I will not undertake to determine; but this I may venture to affirm, that the advantage accruing to the mother country will fall greatly short of the expectations of the ministry; for certain it is, our whole substance does already in a manner flow to Great Britain and that whatsoever contributes to lessen our importations must be hurtful to their manufacturers. And the eyes of our people, already beginning to open, will perceive, that many luxuries which we lavish our substance to Great Britain for, can well be dispensed with whilst the necessaries of life are (mostly) to be had within ourselves. This consequently will introduce frugality, and be a necessary stimulation to industry. If Great Britain therefore loads her manufactures with heavy taxes, will it not facilitate these measures? They will not compel us I think to give our money for their exports whether we will or no, and certain I am none of their traders will part from them without a valuable consideration. Where then is the utility of these restrictions?

As to the Stamp Act, taken in a single view, one, and the first bad consequence attending it I take to be this: our courts of judicature must inevitably be shut up. For it is impossible (or next of kin to it) under our present circumstances that the Act of Parliament can be complied with were we ever so willing to enforce the execution; for not to say, which alone would be sufficient, that we have not money to pay the Stamps, there are many other cogent reasons to prevent it. And if a stop be put to our judicial proceedings I fancy the merchants of Great Britain trading to the colonies will not be among the last to wish for a repeal of it.

TO CAPTAIN JOSIAH THOMPSON

Mount Vernon, July 2, 1766

With this letter comes a Negro (Tom) which I beg the favor of you to sell, in any of the Islands you may go to, for whatever he will fetch, and bring me in return from him

One Hhd of best Molasses
One Ditto of best Rum
One Barrel of Lymes, if good and Cheap

One Pot of Tamarinds, contg. about 10 lbs.
Two small Do of mixed Sweetmeats, abt. 5 lb. each.
And the residue, much or little, in good old Spirits.

That this fellow is both a rogue and a runaway (tho' he was by
no means remarkable for the former, and never practised the
latter till of late) I shall not pretend to deny. But that he is exceedingly healthy, strong, and good at the hoe, the whole neighborhood can testify.

TO GEORGE MASON

Mount Vernon, April 5, 1769

At a time when our lordly masters in Great Britain will be
satisfied with nothing less than the deprivation of American freedom, it seems highly necessary that some thing should be done to
avert the stroke and maintain the liberty which we have derived
from our ancestors; but the manner of doing it to answer the purpose effectually is the point in question.

That no man should scruple, or hesitate a moment to use arms
in defence of so valuable a blessing, on which all the good and
evil of life depends, is clearly my opinion; yet arms I would beg
leave to add, should be the last resource. Addresses to the throne,
and remonstrances to parliament, we have already, it is said,
proved the inefficacy of; how far then their attention to our rights
and privileges is to be awakened or alarmed by starving their
trade and manufacturers, remains to be tried.

The northern colonies, it appears, are endeavoring to adopt the
scheme. In my opinion it is a good one, and must be attended
with salutary effects, provided it can be carried pretty generally
into execution. But how far it is practicable to do so, I will not
take upon me to determine. That there will be difficulties attending the execution of it everywhere, from clashing interests, and
selfish designing men (ever attentive to their own gain, and
watchful of every turn that can assist their lucrative views, in preference to any other consideration) cannot be denied. In the tobacco colonies where the trade is so diffused, and in a manner
wholly conducted by factors for their principals at home, these
difficulties are certainly enhanced, but I think not insurmountably
increased, if the gentlemen in their several counties would be at
some pains to explain matters to the people. . . . The prohibited

goods could be vended to none but the non-associator, or those who would pay no regard to their association; both of whom ought to be stigmatized, and made the objects of public reproach.

TO ROBERT CARY & COMPANY

Mount Vernon, July 25, 1769

If there are any articles contained in either of the respective invoices (paper only excepted) which are taxed by Act of Parliament for the purpose of raising a revenue in America, it is my express desire and request that they may not be sent, as I have very heartily entered into an Association not to import any article which now is or hereafter shall be taxed for this purpose until the said Act or Acts are repealed. I am therefore particular in mentioning this matter as I am fully determined to adhere religiously to it, and may perhaps have wrote for some things unwittingly which may be under these circumstances.

TO ROBERT CARY & COMPANY

Mount Vernon, July 20, 1771

Our Association in Virginia for the non-importation of goods is now at an end except against tea, paper, glass, and painters' colors of foreign manufacture. You will please, therefore, to be careful that none of the glass, paper, etc., contained in my invoices, are those kinds which are subject to the duty imposed by Parliament for the purpose of raising a revenue in America.

TO GEORGE WILLIAM FAIRFAX

Williamsburg, June 10, 1774

The Ministry may rely on it that Americans will never be taxed without their own consent. The cause of Boston now is and ever will be considered as the cause of America (not that we approve their conduct in destroying the tea). We shall not suffer ourselves to be sacrificed piecemeal though god only knows what is to become of us, threatened as we are with so many hovering evils as hang over us at present; having a cruel and blood thirsty enemy upon our backs, the Indians, between whom and our frontier inhabitants many skirmishes have happened, and with whom a general war is inevitable, whilst those from whom we have a right to seek protection are endeavoring by every piece of art and despotism to fix the shackles of slavery upon us.

TO BRYAN FAIRFAX

Mount Vernon, July 4, 1774

As to your political sentiments, I would heartily join you in them, so far as relates to a humble and dutiful petition to the throne, provided there was the most distant hope of success. But have we not tried this already? Have we not addressed the Lords, and remonstrated to the Commons? And to what end? Did they deign to look at our petitions? Does it not appear, as clear as the sun in its meridian brightness, that there is a regular, systematic plan formed to fix the right and practice of taxation upon us? Does not the uniform conduct of Parliament for some years past confirm this? Do not all the debates, especially those just brought to us, in the House of Commons on the side of government, expressly declare that America must be taxed in aid of the British funds, and that she has no longer resources within herself? Is there anything to be expected from petitioning after this? Is not the attack upon the liberty and property of the people of Boston, before restitution of the loss to the India Company was demanded, a plain and self-evident proof of what they are aiming at? Do not the subsequent bills (now I dare say acts), for depriving the Massachusetts Bay of its charter, and for transporting offenders into other colonies or to Great Britain for trial, where it is impossible from the nature of the thing that justice can be obtained, convince us that the administration is determined to stick at nothing to carry its point? Ought we not, then, to put our virtue and fortitude to the severest test?

TO BRYAN FAIRFAX

Mount Vernon, August 24, 1774

For my own part, I shall not undertake to say where the line between Great Britain and the colonies should be drawn; but I am clearly of opinion, that one ought to be drawn, and our rights clearly ascertained. I could wish, I own, that the dispute had been left to posterity to determine, but the crisis is arrived when we must assert our rights, or submit to every imposition that can be heaped upon us, till custom and use shall make us as tame and abject slaves as the blacks we rule over with such arbitrary sway.

TO CAPTAIN ROBERT MACKENZIE

Philadelphia, October 9, 1774

. . . give me leave to add, and I think I can announce it as a fact, that it is not the wish or interest of that government, or any other upon this continent, separately or collectively, to set up for independency; but this you may at the same time rely on, that none of them will ever submit to the loss of those valuable rights and privileges, which are essential to the happiness of every free state, and without which, life, liberty, and property are rendered totally insecure.

2
Revolutionary General, 1775-1783

TO MARTHA WASHINGTON

Philadelphia, June 18, 1775

It has been determined in Congress, that the whole army raised for the defence of the American cause shall be put under my care, and that it is necessary for me to proceed immediately to Boston to take upon me the command of it. You may believe me, my dear Patsy, when I assure you, in the most solemn manner that, so far from seeking this appointment, I have used every endeavor in my power to avoid it, not only from my unwillingness to part with you and the family, but from a consciousness of its being a trust too great for my capacity, and that I should enjoy more real happiness in one month with you at home, than I have the most distant prospect of finding abroad, if my stay were to be seven times seven years. But as it has been a kind of destiny that has thrown me upon this service, I shall hope that my undertaking is designed to answer some good purpose. . . . It was utterly out of my power to refuse the appointment without exposing my character to such censures, as would have reflected dishonor upon myself, and given pain to my friends. This, I am sure, could not, and ought not, to be pleasing to you, and must have lessened me considerably in my own esteem. I shall rely, therefore, confidently on that Providence, which has heretofore preserved and been bountiful to me, not doubting but that I shall return safe to you in the fall.

TO RICHARD HENRY LEE

Cambridge, July 10, 1775

The abuses in this army, I fear, are considerable, and the new modelling of it, in the face of an enemy from whom we every hour expect an attack, is exceedingly difficult and dangerous. If things therefore should not turn out as the Congress would wish, I hope they will make proper allowances. I can only promise and assure them, that my whole time is devoted to their service.

GENERAL ORDERS

Cambridge, July 15, 1775

Notwithstanding the orders already given, the General hears with astonishment, that not only Soldiers, but Officers unauthorized are continually conversing with the Officers and Sentrys of the enemy; any Officer, Non-Commissioned Officer or Soldier, or any person whatsover, who is detected holding any conversation, or carrying on any correspondence with any of the Officers or Sentrys of the advanced posts of the enemy, will be immediately brought before a General Court Martial, and punished with the utmost severity.

TO THE MASSACHUSETTS LEGISLATURE

Cambridge, July 31, 1775

The great advantage the enemy has, of transporting troops, by being master of the sea, will enable them to harass us by diversions of this kind; and should we be tempted to pursue them upon every alarm, the Army must either be so weakened as to expose it to destruction, or a great part of the coast be still left unprotected. Nor, indeed, does it appear to me, that such pursuit would be attended with the least effect. The first notice of such an incursion would be its actual execution; and long before any troops could reach the scene of action, the enemy would have an opportunity to accomplish their purpose and retire.

GENERAL ORDERS

Cambridge, August 22, 1775

The General does not mean to discourage the practice of bathing whilst the weather is warm enough to continue it, but he expressly forbids any persons doing it at or near the bridge in Cambridge, where it has been observed and complained of that many men, lost to all sense of decency and common modesty, are running about naked upon the bridge, whilst passengers, and even ladies of the first fashion in the neighborhood, are passing over it, as if they meant to glory in their shame.

TO THE INHABITANTS OF CANADA

Cambridge, September, 1775

Above all we rejoice that our enemies have been deceived with regard to you. They have persuaded themselves, they have even dared to say, that the Canadians were not capable of distinguishing between the blessings of liberty and the wretchedness of slavery; that gratifying the vanity of a little circle of nobility would blind the eyes of the people of Canada. By such artifices they hoped to bend you to their views; but they have been deceived. Instead of finding in you that poverty of soul and baseness of spirit, they see with a chagrin equal to our joy, that you are enlightened, generous, and virtuous; that you will not renounce your own rights, or serve as instruments to deprive your fellow subjects of theirs. Come then, my brethren, unite with us in an indissoluble Union. Let us run together to the same goal. We have taken up arms in defence of our liberty, our property, our wives and our children. We are determined to preserve them or die. We look forward with pleasure to that day not far remote (we hope) when the inhabitants of America shall have one sentiment and the full enjoyment of the blessings of a free government.

TO COLONEL BENEDICT ARNOLD

Cambridge, January 27, 1776

I received the melancholy account of the unfortunate attack on the city of Quebec, attended with the fall of General Montgomery and other brave officers and men, and of your being wounded.

TO JOSEPH REED

Cambridge, February 1, 1776

The account given of the behavior of the men under General Montgomery is exactly consonant to the opinion I have formed of these people. . . . Place them behind a parapet, a breastwork, stone wall or anything that will afford them shelter, and, from their knowledge of a firelock, they will give a good account of their enemy; but . . . they will not march boldly up to a work, nor stand exposed in a plain.

TO THE PRESIDENT OF CONGRESS

Cambridge, February 9, 1776

To expect . . . the same service from raw, and undisciplined recruits as from veteran soldiers, is to expect what never did, and perhaps never will happen. Men who are familiarized to danger meet it without shrinking, whereas those who have never seen service often apprehend danger where no danger is. Three things prompt men to a regular discharge of their duty in time of action: natural bravery, hope of reward, and fear of punishment. The two first are common to the untutored and the disciplined soldiers; but the latter most obviously distinguishes the one from the other. A coward, when taught to believe, that if he breaks his ranks and abandons his colors, will be punished with death by his own party, will take his chance against the enemy; but the man who thinks little of the one, and is fearful of the other, acts from present feelings regardless of the consequences.

GENERAL ORDERS

New York, July 2, 1776

The fate of unborn millions will now depend, under God, on the courage and conduct of this army. Our cruel and unrelenting enemy leaves us no choice but a brave resistance or the most abject submission. This is all we can expect. We have therefore to resolve to conquer or die. Our own country's honor, all call upon us for a vigorous and manly exertion, and if we now shamefully fall, we shall become infamous to the whole world. Let us therefore rely upon the goodness of the cause, and the aid of the supreme Being, in whose hands victory is, to animate and encourage us to great and noble actions. The eyes of all our countrymen are now upon us, and we shall have their blessings, and praises, if happily we are the instruments of saving them from the tyranny meditated against them. Let us . . . show the world that a freeman contending for LIBERTY on his own ground is superior to any slavish mercenary on earth.

TO MAJOR GENERAL ARTEMAS WARD

New York, July 9, 1776

The inclosed Declaration will show you, that Congress at length, impelled by necessity, have dissolved the connection between the American colonies and Great Britain, and declared them *free* and *independent states;* and in compliance with their order, I am to request you will cause this Declaration to be immediately proclaimed at the head of the Continental Regiments in the Massachusetts Bay.

GENERAL ORDERS

New York, July 25, 1776

It is with inexpressible concern, the General sees soldiers fighting in the cause of liberty and their country, committing crimes most destructive to the army, and which in all other armies are punished with death. What a shame and reproach will it be if [British] soldiers fighting to enslave us, for two pence, or three pence a day, should be more regular, watchful and sober, than men who are contending for everything that is dear and valuable in life.

TO THE PRESIDENT OF CONGRESS

New York, September 8, 1776

History, our own experience, the advice of our ablest friends in Europe, the fears of the enemy, and even the declarations of Congress demonstrate, that on our side the war should be defensive. It has even been called a War of Posts.

TO THE PRESIDENT OF CONGRESS

Heights of Harlem, September 24, 1776

To place any dependence upon the militia is, assuredly, resting upon a broken staff. Men just dragged from the tender scenes of domestic life; unaccustomed to the din of arms; totally unacquainted with every kind of military skill, which being followed by a want of confidence in themselves, when opposed to troops regularly trained, disciplined, and appointed, superior in knowledge, and superior in arms, makes them timid, and ready to fly from their own shadows. Besides, the sudden change in their manner of living (particularly in the lodging), bring on sickness in many, impatience in all, and such an unconquerable desire of returning to their respective homes that it produces not only shameful, but scandalous desertions among themselves, but infuses the like spirit in others. Again, men accustomed to unbounded freedom, and no control, cannot brook the restraint which is indispensably necessary to the good order and government of any army.

GENERAL ORDERS

Morristown, January 21, 1777

The General is very sorry to find that the late order allowing . . . plunder . . . has been so mistaken by some and abused by others. This indulgence was granted to scouting parties only, as a reward for the extraordinary fatigues, hardship, and danger they were exposed to upon those parties. The General never meant, nor had any idea, that any of our own or enemy's stores, found at any evacuated post, were to be considered as the property of those that first marched in.

GENERAL ORDERS

Morristown, May 8, 1777

As few vices are attended with more pernicious consequences in civil life, so there are none more fatal in a military one than that of GAM[BL]ING, which often brings disgrace and ruin upon officers, and injury and punishment upon the soldiery. And reports prevailing, which, it is to be feared are too well founded, that this destructive vice has spread its baneful influence in the army, and, in a peculiar manner, to the prejudice of the recruiting service—The Commander in Chief, in the most pointed and explicit terms, forbids ALL officers and soldiers, playing at cards, dice, or at any games, except those of EXERCISE, for diversion; it being impossible, if the practice be allowed at all, to discriminate between innocent play for amusement, and criminal gam[bl]ing for pecuniary and sordid purposes.

TO RICHARD HENRY LEE

Morristown, May 17, 1777

I take the liberty to ask you, what Congress expects I am to do with the many foreigners they have, at different times, promoted to the rank of Field Officers? In making these appointments, it is much to be feared that all the circumstances attending are not taken into consideration. To oblige the adventurers of a nation whom we want to interest in our cause, may be one inducement; and to get rid of their importunity, another; but this is viewing the matter by halves, or one side only. These men have no attachment or ties to the country, further than interest binds them; they have no influence, and are ignorant of the language they are to receive and give orders in, consequently great trouble or much confusion must follow. But this is not the worst. They have not the smallest chance to recruit others, and our officers think it exceedingly hard, after they have toiled in this service, and probably sustained many losses, to have strangers put over them whose merit, perhaps, is not equal to their own, but whose effrontery will take no denial.

GENERAL ORDERS

Middlebrook, May 31, 1777

It is much to be lamented that the foolish and scandalous practise of *profane swearing* is exceedingly prevalent in the American army. Officers of every rank are bound to discourage it, first by their example, and then by punishing offenders. As a means to abolish this, and every other species of immorality, Brigadiers are enjoined to take effectual care to have divine service duly performed in their respective brigades.

TO CHEVALIER D'ANMOURS

Middlebrook, June 19, 1777

An immediate declaration of war [by France] against Britain, in all probability, could not fail to extricate us from all our difficulties, and to cement the bond of friendship so firmly between France and America as to produce the most permanent advantages to both. Certainly nothing can be more the true interest of France than to have a weight of such magnitude as America taken out of the scale of British power and opulence and thrown into that of her own.

TO JOHN AUGUSTINE WASHINGTON

Germantown, August 5, 1777

I have, from the first, been among those few who never built much upon a French war. I ever did, and still do think, they never meant more than to give us a kind of underhand assistance; that is, to supply us with arms, etc., for our money and trade. This may indeed, if Great Britain has spirit and strength to resent it, bring on a war; but the declaration, if on either side must, I am convinced, come from the last mentioned power.

GENERAL ORDERS

Wilmington, September 4, 1777

Notwithstanding all the cautions, the earnest requests, and the positive orders of the Commander in Chief, to prevent *our own army* from plundering *our own friends* and *fellow citizens,* yet to his astonishment and grief, fresh complaints are made to him that so wicked, infamous and cruel a practice is still continued, and that too in circumstances most distressing: where the wretched inhabitants, dreading the enemy's vengeance for their adherence to our cause, have left all, and fled to us for refuge! We complain of the cruelty and barbarity of our enemies; but does it equal ours? They sometimes spare the property of their *friends.* But some amongst us, beyond expression barbarous, rob even *them!* Why did we assemble in arms? Was it not, in one capital point, to protect the property of our countrymen? And shall we to our eternal reproach, be the first to pillage and destroy? Will no motives of humanity, of zeal, interest and of honor, restrain the violence of the soldiers, or induce officers to keep so strict a watch over the ill-disposed, as effectually to prevent the execution of their evil designs, and the gratification of their savage inclinations? Or, if these powerful motives are too weak, will they pay no regard to their own safety? How many noble designs have miscarried, how many victories have been lost, how many armies ruined, by an indulgence of soldiers in plundering?

TO THE PRESIDENT OF CONGRESS

Whitemarsh, November 17, 1777

I am informed . . . that reflections have been thrown out against this army, for not being more active and enterprising than, in the opinion of some, they ought to have been. If the charge is just, the best way to account for it will be to refer you to the returns of our strength and those which I can produce for the enemy, and to the enclosed abstract of the clothing now actually wanting for the army, and then I think the wonder will be, how they keep the field at all, in tents, at this season of the year.

TO THE PRESIDENT OF CONGRESS

Near the Gulph, December 14, 1777

I have been well aware of the prevalent jealousy of military power, and that this has been considered as an evil much to be apprehended even by the best and most sensible among us. Under this idea, I have been cautious and wished to avoid as much as possible any act that might improve it. . . . The people at large are governed much by custom. To acts of legislation or civil authority they have been ever taught to yield a willing obedience without reasoning about their propriety. On those of military power, whether immediate or derived originally from another source, they have ever looked with a jealous and suspicious eye.

GENERAL ORDERS

Valley Forge, January 20, 1778

The General positively forbids the burning of the farmer's fences; he enjoins it upon all officers to use their endeavors to prevent it and bring to severe punishment all those who shall offend herein.

GENERAL ORDERS

Valley Forge, March 1, 1778

The Commander in Chief again takes occasion to return his warmest thanks to the virtuous officers and soldiery of this army for that persevering fidelity and zeal which they have uniformly manifested in all their conduct. Their fortitude not only under the common hardships incident to a military life, but also under the additional sufferings to which the peculiar situation of these States have exposed them, clearly proves them worthy the enviable privilege of contending for the rights of human nature, the *freedom and independence* of their country. The recent instance of uncomplaining patience during the scarcity of provisions in camp is a fresh proof that they possess in an eminent degree the spirit of soldiers and the magnanimity of patriots. The few refractory individuals who disgrace themselves by murmurs it is to be hoped have repented such unmanly behavior, and resolved to emulate the noble example of their associates upon every trial which the customary casualties of war may hereafter throw in their way. . . . Surely we who are free citizens in arms engaged in a struggle for everything valuable in society and partaking in the glorious task of laying the foundation of an *Empire*, should scorn effeminately to shrink under those accidents and rigors of war which mercenary hirelings fighting in the cause of lawless ambition, rapine and devastation, encounter with cheerfulness and alacrity. We should not be merely equal, we should be superior to them in every qualification that dignifies the man or the soldier in proportion as the motive from which we act and the final hopes of our toils are superior to theirs.

TO JOHN BANISTER

Valley Forge, April 21, 1778

Men may speculate as they will; they may talk of patriotism; they may draw a few examples from ancient story, of great achievements performed by its influence; but whoever builds upon it, as a sufficient basis for conducting a long and bloody war will find themselves deceived in the end. We must take the passions of men as nature has given them, and those principles as a guide which are generally the rule of action. I do not mean to exclude altogether the idea of patriotism. I know it exists, and I know it has done much in the present contest. But I will venture to assert that a great and lasting war can never be supported on this principle alone. It must be aided by a prospect of interest or some reward. For a time, it may, of itself push men to action, to bear much, to encounter difficulties; but it will not endure unassisted by interest.

TO REVEREND ALEXANDER MCWHORTER

Fredericksburg, October 12, 1778

There are now under sentence of death, in the provost, a Farnsworth and Blair, convicted of being spies from the enemy, and of publishing counterfeit Continental currency. It is hardly to be doubted but that these unfortunate men are acquainted with many facts respecting the enemy's affairs and their intentions, which we have not been able to bring them to acknowledge. Besides the humanity of affording them the benefit of your profession, it may . . . answer another valuable purpose. And while it serves to prepare them for the other world, it will naturally lead to the intelligence we want in your inquiries into the condition of their spiritual concerns. . . . When you have collected in the course of your attendance such information as they can give, you will transmit the whole to me.

TO HENRY LAURENS

Fredericksburg, November 14, 1778

The question of the Canadian expedition in the form it now stands appears to me one of the most interesting that has hitherto agitated our national deliberations. I have one objection to it . . . which is in my estimation, insurmountable, and alarms all my feelings for the true and permanent interests of my country. This is the introduction of a large body of French troops into Canada, and putting them in possession of the capital of that province, attached to them by all the ties of blood, habits, manners, religion and former connection of government. I fear this would be too great a temptation to be resisted by any power actuated by the common maxims of national policy. Let us realize for a moment the striking advantages France would derive from the possession of Canada—the acquisition of an extensive territory abounding in supplies for the use of her islands; the opening [of] a vast source of the most beneficial commerce with the Indian nations, which she might then monopolize; the having ports of her own on this continent independent of the precarious good will of an ally; the engrossing the whole trade of Newfoundland whenever she pleased, the finest nursery of seamen in the world; the security afforded to her islands; and finally, the facility of awing and controlling these states, the natural and most formidable rival of every maritime power in Europe. Canada would be a solid acquisition to France on all these accounts and because of the numerous inhabitants, subjects to her by inclination, who would aid in preserving it under her power against the attempt of every other.

France, acknowledged for some time past the most powerful monarchy in Europe by land, able now to dispute the empire of the sea with Great Britain, and if joined with Spain, I may say certainly superior, possessed of New Orleans on our right, Canada on our left, and seconded by the numerous tribes of Indians on our rear from one extremity to another, a people so generally friendly to her and whom she knows so well how to conciliate— [France] would, it is much to be apprehended, have it in her power to give law to these states.

TO MARQUIS DE LAFAYETTE

Middlebrook, March 8, 1779

We are happy in the repeated assurances and proofs of the friendship of our great and good Ally whom we hope and trust, ere this, may be congratulated on the birth of a Prince; and on the joy which the nation must derive from an instance of royal felicity. We also flatter ourselves that before this period the Kings of Spain and the two Sicilies may be greeted as Allies of the United States; and we are not a little pleased to find from good authority, that the solicitations and offers of the Court of Great Britain to the Empress of Russia have been rejected with *disdain;* nor are we to be displeased, that overtures from the City of Amsterdam for entering into a commercial connection with us, have been made in such open and pointed terms. Such favorable sentiments in so many powerful Princes and States cannot but be considered in a very honorable, interesting, and pleasing point of view, by all those who have struggled with difficulties and misfortune to maintain the rights and secure the liberties of their country.

TO GEORGE MASON

Middlebrook, March 27, 1779

I view things very differently, I fear, from what people in general do who seem to think the contest is at an end; and to make money, and get places, the only things now remaining to do. I have seen without despondency (even for a moment) the hours which America have styled her gloomy ones, but I have beheld no day since the commencement of hostilities that I have thought her liberties in such eminent danger as at present. Friends and foes seem now to combine to pull down the goodly fabric we have hitherto been raising at the expense of so much time, blood, and treasure; and unless the bodies politic will exert themselves to bring things back to first principles, correct abuses, and punish our internal foes, inevitable ruin must follow. Indeed we seem to be verging so fast to destruction that I am filled with sensations to which I have been a stranger till within these three months. It is now consistent with the views of the speculators, various tribes of money makers, and stock jobbers of all denominations, to continue the war for their own private emolument, without considering that their avarice, and thirst for gain must plunge everything (including themselves) in one common ruin.

SPEECH TO THE DELAWARE CHIEFS

Middlebrook, May 12, 1779

Brothers: I am a Warrior. My words are few and plain; but I will make good what I say. 'Tis my business to destroy all the enemies of these States and to protect their friends. You have seen how we have withstood the English for four years; and how their great armies have dwindled away and come to very little; and how what remains of them in this part of our great country are glad to stay upon two or three little islands, where the waters and their ships hinder us from going to destroy them. The English, Brothers, are a boasting people. They talk of doing a good deal; but they do very little. They fly away on their ships from one part of our country to another; but as soon as our warriors get together they leave it and go to some other part. They took Boston and Philadelphia, two of our greatest towns; but when they saw our warriors in a great body ready to fall upon them, they were forced to leave them.

Brothers: We have till lately fought the English all alone. Now the great King of France is become our good brother and Ally. He has taken up the hatchet with us, and we have sworn never to bury it till we have punished the English and made them sorry for all the wicked things they had in their hearts to do against these States. And there are other great Kings and Nations on the other side of the big waters, who love us and wish us well, and will not suffer the English to hurt us.

Brothers: Listen well to what I tell you and let it sink deep into your hearts. We love our friends, and will be faithful to them, as long as they will be faithful to us. We are sure our good brothers the Delawares will always be so. But we have sworn to take vengeance on our enemies, and on false friends.

Brothers: You do well to wish to learn our arts and ways of life, and above all, the religion of Jesus Christ. These will make you a greater and happier people than you are. Congress will do everything they can to assist you. . . .

TO PRESIDENT JOSEPH REED

Morristown, May 28, 1780

The combined fleets of France and Spain last year were greatly superior of those of the enemy. The enemy nevertheless sustained no material damage, and at the close of the campaign have given a very important blow to our allies. What are we to expect will be the case if there should be another campaign? In all probability the advantage will be on the side of the English and then what would become of America? We ought not to deceive ourselves. The maritime resources of Great Britain are more substantial and real than those of France and Spain united. Her commerce is more extensive than that of both her rivals; and it is an axiom that the nation which has the most extensive commerce will always have the most powerful marine.

GENERAL ORDERS

Orangetown, September 26, 1780

Treason of the blackest dye was yesterday discovered! General Arnold who commanded at West Point, lost to every sentiment of honor, or public and private obligation, was about to deliver up that important Post into the hands of the enemy. Such an event must have given the American cause a deadly wound if not a fatal stab. Happily the treason has been timely discovered to prevent the fatal misfortune. The providential train of circumstances which led to it affords the most convincing proof that the liberties of America are the object of divine protection.

At the same time that the treason is to be regretted the General cannot help congratulating the Army on the happy discovery. Our enemies, despairing of carrying their point by force, are practising every base art to effect by bribery and corruption what they cannot accomplish in a manly way.

Great honor is due to the American Army that this is the first instance of treason of the kind, where many were to be expected from the nature of the dispute, and nothing is so bright an ornament in the character of the American soldiers as their having been proof against all the arts and seduction of an insidious enemy.

GENERAL ORDERS

New Windsor, January 30, 1781

History is full of examples of armies suffering with patience extremities of distress which exceed those we have suffered, and this in the cause of ambition and conquest, not in that of the rights of humanity, of their country, of their families, of themselves. Shall we who aspire to the distinction of a patriot army, who are contending for everything precious in society against everything hateful and degrading in slavery; shall we who call ourselves citizens discover less constancy and military virtue than the mercenary instruments of ambition? Those [mutineers] who in the present instance have stained the honor of the American soldiery and sullied the reputation of patient virtue for which they have been so long eminent, can only atone for the pusillanimous defection by a life devoted to a zealous and exemplary discharge of their duty. Persuaded that the greater part were influenced by the pernicious advice of a few who probably have been paid by the enemy to betray their associates, the General is happy in the lenity shown in the execution of only two of the most guilty, after compelling the whole to an unconditional surrender, and he flatters himself no similar instance will hereafter disgrace our military history.

TO LUND WASHINGTON

New Windsor, April 30, 1781

I am very sorry to hear of your loss; I am a little sorry to hear of my own; but that which gives me most concern is, that you should go on board the enemy's vessels and furnish them with refreshments. It would have been a less painful circumstance to me, to have heard, that in consequence of your non-compliance with their request, they had burnt my house and laid the plantation in ruins. You ought to have considered yourself as my representative, and should have reflected on the bad example of communicating with the enemy, and making a voluntary offer of refreshments to them with a view to prevent a conflagration.

It was not in your power, I acknowledge, to prevent them from sending a flag on shore, and you did right to meet it; but you should, in the same instant that the business of it was unfolded, have declared, explicitly, that it was improper for you to yield to the request; after which, if they had proceeded to help themselves, *by force,* you could but have submitted (and being unprovided for defense), this was to be preferred to a feeble opposition which only serves as a pretext to burn and destroy.

I am thoroughly persuaded that you acted from your best judgment; and believe, that your desire to preserve my property, and rescue the buildings from impending danger, were your governing motives. But to go on board their vessels; carry them refreshments; commune with a parcel of plundering scoundrels; and request a favor by asking the surrender of my Negroes, was exceedingly ill-judged, and 'tis to be feared, will be unhappy in its consequences, as it will be a precedent for others, and may become a subject of animadversion.

TO THE PRESIDENT OF CONGRESS

York, October 19, 1781

I have the honor to inform Congress that a reduction of the British army under the command of Lord Cornwallis is most happily effected. The unremitting ardor which actuated every officer and soldier in the combined army on this occasion, has principally led to this important event at an earlier period than my most sanguine hopes had induced me to expect.

TO JOHN MITCHELL

Verplank's Point, September 16, 1782

I heartily wish that the general prevailing ideas of peace may not be injurious to us; the appearances, in my opinion, are very equivocal; but one thing we are sure of, and that is that being in a state of perfect preparation for war is the only sure and infallible means of producing peace.

TO MARQUIS DE LAFAYETTE

Newburgh, April 5, 1783

We now stand an independent people, and have yet to learn political tactics. We are placed among the nations of the earth, and have a character to establish; but how we shall acquit ourselves time must discover. The probability, at least I fear it, is that local, or state politics will interfere too much with that more liberal and extensive plan of government which wisdom and foresight, freed from the mist of prejudice, would dictate; and that we shall be guilty of many blunders in treading this boundless theatre before we shall have arrived at any perfection in this art. In a word, that the experience which is purchased at the price of difficulties and distress, will alone convince us that the honor, power, and true interest of this country must be measured by a continental scale; and that every departure therefrom weakens the Union, and may ultimately break the band which holds us together. To avert these evils, to form a Constitution that will give consistency, stability and dignity to the Union, and sufficient powers to the great Council of the nation for general purposes, is a duty which is incumbent upon every man who wishes well to his country, and will meet with my aid as far as it can be rendered in the private walks of life.

FAREWELL ORDERS TO THE ARMIES
OF THE UNITED STATES

Rock Hill, near Princeton, November 2, 1783

Every American officer and soldier must now console himself for any unpleasant circumstances which may have occurred by a recollection of the uncommon scenes in which he has been called to act no inglorious part, and the astonishing events of which he has been a witness, events which have seldom if ever before taken place on the stage of human action, nor can they probably ever happen again. For who has before seen a disciplined army formed at once from such raw materials? Who, that was not a witness, could imagine that the most violent local prejudices would cease so soon, and that men who came from the different parts of the continent, strongly disposed, by the habits of education, to despise and quarrel with each other, would instantly become but one patriotic band of brothers; or who, that was not on the spot, can trace the steps by which such a wonderful revolution has been effected, and such a glorious period put to all our warlike toils?

3
Founding Father, 1785-1788

TO JAMES DUANE

Mount Vernon, April 10, 1785

It is painful, to hear that a State [New York] which used to be the foremost in acts of liberality and its exertion to establish our federal system upon a broad bottom and solid ground, is contracting her ideas, and pointing them to local and independent measures; which, if persevered in, must sap the Constitution of these States (already too weak), destroy our national character, and render us as contemptible in the eyes of Europe as we have it in our power to be respectable.

TO DAVID HUMPHREYS

Mount Vernon, July 25, 1785

As the complexion of European politics seems now to have a tendency to peace, I will say nothing of war. . . . My first wish is to see this plague to mankind banished from off the earth, and the sons and daughters of this world employed in more pleasing and innocent amusements, than in preparing implements and exercising them for the destruction of mankind. Rather than quarrel about territory let the poor, the needy and oppressed of the earth, and those who want land, resort to the fertile plains of our western country, the *second land of promise*, and there dwell in peace, fulfilling the first and great commandment.

TO JAMES MCHENRY

Mount Vernon, August 22, 1785

As I have ever been a friend to adequate powers of Congress, without which it is evident to me we never shall establish a national character, or be considered as on a respectable footing by the powers of Europe, I am sorry I cannot agree with you in senti-ment not to enlarge them for the regulating of commerce. . . . Your arguments against it, principally, that some States may be more benefited than others by a commercial regulation, apply to every matter of general utility; for can there be a case enumer-ated in which this argument has not its force in a greater or less degree? We are either a united people under one head, and for federal purposes; or we are thirteen independent sovereignties, eternally counteracting each other: if the former, whatever such a majority of the States as the Constitution points out, conceives to be for the benefit of the whole, should, in my humble opinion, be submitted to by the minority. Let the southern States always be represented; let them act more in union; let them declare freely and boldly what is for the interest of, and what is preju-dicial to their constituents; and there will, there *must* be an ac-commodating spirit.

TO JAMES WARREN

Mount Vernon, October 7, 1785

The war, as you have very justly observed, has terminated most advantageously for America, and a fair field is presented to our view; but I confess to you freely, my dear sir, that I do not think we possess wisdom or justice enough to cultivate it prop-erly. Illiberality, jealousy, and local policy mix too much in all our public councils for the good government of the Union. In a word, the confederation appears to me to be little more than a shadow without the substance; and Congress a nugatory body, their ordinances being little attended to. To *me*, it is a solecism in politics: indeed it is one of the most extraordinary things in nature, that we should confederate as a nation, and yet be afraid to give the rulers of that nation, who are the creatures of our making, appointed for a limited and short duration, and who are amenable for every action, and recallable at any moment, and are subject to all the evils which they may be instrumental in producing, sufficient powers to order and direct the affairs of the same. By such policy as this the wheels of government are clogged, and our brightest prospects, and that high expectation which was entertained of us by the wondering world, are turned into astonishment; and from the high ground on which we stood, we are descending into the vale of confusion and darkness.

TO CHEVALIER DE LA LUZERNE

Mount Vernon, August 1, 1786

Our internal governments are daily acquiring strength. The laws have their fullest energy; justice is well administered; robbery, violence or murder is not heard of from New Hampshire to Georgia. The people at large (as far as I can learn) are more industrious than they were before the war. Economy begins, partly from necessity and partly from choice and habit, to prevail. The seeds of population are scattered over an immense tract of western country. In the old States, which were the theatres of hostility, it is wonderful to see how soon the ravages of war are repaired. Houses are rebuilt, fields enclosed, stocks of cattle which were destroyed are replaced, and many a desolated territory assumes again the cheerful appearance of cultivation. In many places the vestiges of conflagration and ruin are hardly to be traced. The arts of peace, such as clearing rivers, building bridges, and establishing conveniences for travelling, etc., are assiduously promoted. In short, the foundation of a great Empire is laid, and I please myself with a persuasion, that Providence will not leave its work imperfect.

TO THE SECRETARY FOR FOREIGN AFFAIRS

Mount Vernon, August 1, 1786

Our affairs are drawing rapidly to a crisis. . . . What the event will be, is also beyond the reach of my foresight. We have errors to correct; we have probably had too good an opinion of human nature in forming our confederation. Experience has taught us, that men will not adopt and carry into execution measures the best calculated for their own good, without the intervention of a coercive power. I do not conceive we can exist long as a nation without having lodged somewhere a power, which will pervade the whole Union in as energetic a manner as the authority of the State governments extends over the several states.

TO DAVID HUMPHREYS

Mount Vernon, October 22, 1786

But for God's sake tell me what is the cause of all these commotions [Shays' rebellion]? Do they proceed from licentiousness, British-influence disseminated by the tories, or real grievances which admit of redress? If the latter, why were they delayed 'till the public mind had become so much agitated? If the former why are not the powers of government tried at once? It is as well to be without, as not to live under their exercise. Commotions of this sort, like snow-balls, gather strength as they roll, if there is no opposition in the way to divide and crumble them.

TO HENRY LEE

Mount Vernon, October 31, 1786

My humble opinion is that there is a call for decision. Know precisely what the insurgents aim at. If they have *real* grievances, redress them if possible; or acknowledge the justice of them, and your inability to do it in the present moment. If they have not, employ the force of government against them at once. If this is inadequate, *all* will be convinced that the superstructure is bad, or wants support. To be more exposed in the eyes of the world, and more contemptible than we are, is hardly possible.

TO JAMES MADISON

Mount Vernon, November 5, 1786

Without some alteration in our political creed, the superstructure we have been seven years raising at the expence of so much blood and treasure, must fall. We are fast verging to anarchy and confusion!

TO HENRY KNOX

Mount Vernon, December 26, 1786

I feel, my dear Genl. Knox, infinitely more than I can express to you, for the disorders which have arisen in these States. Good God! Who besides a tory could have foreseen, or a Briton predicted them! Were these people wiser than others, or did they judge of us from the corruption and depravity of their own hearts? The latter I am persuaded was the case, and that notwithstanding the boasted virtue of America, we are far gone in everything ignoble and bad.

TO HENRY KNOX

Mount Vernon, April 2, 1787

I see, or think I see, reasons for and against my attendance [at the Philadelphia] Convention so near an equilibrium, as will cause me to determine upon either with diffidence. One of the reasons against it, is, an apprehension that all the States will not appear; and that some of them, being unwillingly drawn into the measure, will send their delegates so fettered as to embarrass, and perhaps render nugatory the whole proceedings. In either of these circumstances, that is, a partial representation, or cramped powers, I should not like to be a sharer in this business. If the delegates come with such powers as will enable the Convention to probe the defects of the Constitution to the bottom, and point out radical cures, it would be an honorable employment; but otherwise it is desirable to avoid it.

TO THOMAS JEFFERSON

Philadelphia, May 30, 1787

The business of this Convention is as yet too much in embryo to form any opinion of the result. Much is expected from it by some; but little by others; and nothing by a few. That something is necessary, all will agree; for the situation of the general Government (if it can be called a government) is shaken to its foundation, and liable to be overset by every blast. In a word, it is at an end, and unless a remedy is soon applied, anarchy and confusion will inevitably ensue.

TO MARQUIS DE LAFAYETTE

Philadelphia, June 6, 1787

The pressure of the public voice was so loud, I could not resist the call to a convention of the States which is to determine whether we are to have a Government of respectability under which life, liberty, and property will be secured to us, or are to submit to one which may be the result of chance or the moment, springing perhaps from anarchy and confusion, and dictated perhaps by some aspiring demagogue who will not consult the interest of his country so much as his own ambitious views. What may be the result of the present deliberation is more than I am able, at present, if I was at liberty, to inform you.

TO PATRICK HENRY

Mount Vernon, September 24, 1787

In the first moment after my return I take the liberty of sending you a copy of the Constitution which the Federal Convention has submitted to the people of these States. I accompany it with no observations; your own judgment will at once discover the good and the exceptionable parts of it, and your experience of the difficulties which have ever arisen when attempts have been made to reconcile such variety of interests and local prejudices as pervade the several States will render explanation unnecessary. I wish the Constitution which is offered had been made more perfect, but I sincerely believe it is the best that could be obtained at this time; and, as a constitutional door is opened for amendment hereafter, the adoption of it under the present circumstances of the Union, is in my opinion desirable.

TO MARQUIS DE LAFAYETTE

Mount Vernon, February 7, 1788

It appears to me . . . little short of a miracle, that the delegates from so many different States . . . should unite in forming a system of national Government, so little liable to well founded objections. Nor am I yet such an enthusiastic, partial or undiscriminating admirer of it, as not to perceive it is tinctured with some real (though not radical) defects. . . . My Creed is simply:

1st. That the general Government is not invested with more powers than are indispensably necessary to perform the functions of a good government; and, consequently, that no objection ought to be made against the quantity of power delegated to it.

2ly. That these powers . . . are so distributed among the Legislative, Executive, and Judicial Branches, into which the general government is arranged, that it can never be in danger of degenerating into a monarchy, an oligarchy, an aristocracy, or any other despotic or oppressive form, so long as there shall remain any virtue in the body of the people.

TO MARQUIS DE LAFAYETTE

Mount Vernon, June 18, 1788

I expect that many blessings will be attributed to our new government which are now taking their rise from that industry and frugality into the practice of which the people have been forced from necessity. I really believe that there never was so much labor and economy to be found before in the country as at the present moment. If they persist in the habits they are acquiring, the good effects will soon be distinguishable. When the people shall find themselves secure under an energetic government, when foreign nations shall be disposed to give us equal advantages in commerce from dread of retaliation, when the burdens of war shall be in a manner done away by the sale of western lands, when the seeds of happiness which are sown here shall begin to expand themselves, and when everyone (under his own vine and fig-tree) shall begin to taste the fruits of freedom, then all these blessings (for all these blessings will come) will be referred to the fostering influence of the new government, whereas many causes will have conspired to produce them.

TO BENJAMIN LINCOLN

Mount Vernon, June 29, 1788

No one *can* rejoice more than I do at every step the people of this great country take to preserve the Union, establish good order and government, and to render the nation happy at home and respectable abroad. No country upon earth ever had it more in its power to attain these blessings than United America. Wondrously strange then, and much to be regretted indeed would it be, were we to neglect the means, and to depart from the road which Providence has pointed us to, so plainly; I cannot believe it will ever come to pass. The great Governor of the Universe has led us too long and too far on the road to happiness and glory, to forsake us in the midst of it. By folly and improper conduct, proceeding from a variety of causes, we may now and then get bewildered; but I hope and trust that there is good sense and virtue enough left to recover the right path before we shall be entirely lost.

TO BENJAMIN LINCOLN

Mount Vernon, October 26, 1788

I would willingly pass over in silence that part of your letter, in which you mention the persons who are candidates for the two first offices in the Executive, if I did not fear the omission might seem to betray a want of confidence. . . . Every personal consideration conspires to rivet me (if I may use the expression) to retirement. At my time of life, and under my circumstances, nothing in this world can ever draw me from it, unless it be a *conviction* that the partiality of my countrymen had made my services absolutely necessary, joined to a *fear* that my refusal might induce a belief that I preferred the conservation of my own reputation and private ease to the good of my country. After all, if I should conceive myself in a manner constrained to accept, I call Heaven to witness, that this very act would be the greatest sacrifice of my personal feelings and wishes that ever I have been called upon to make. It would be to forego repose and domestic enjoyment, for trouble, perhaps for public obloquy. For I should consider myself as entering upon an unexplored field, enveloped on every side with clouds and darkness.

4

First President of the United States, 1789–1797

TO EDWARD RUTLEDGE

New York, May 5, 1789

I greatly apprehend that my countrymen will expect too much from me. I fear, if the issue of public measures should not correspond with their sanguine expectations, they will turn the extravagant (and I may say undue) praises which they are heaping upon me at this moment, into equally extravagant (though I will fondly hope unmerited) censures. So much is expected, so many untoward circumstances may intervene, in such a new and critical situation, that I feel an insuperable diffidence in my own abilities. I feel, in the execution of the duties of my arduous office, how much I shall stand in need of the countenance and aid of every friend to myself, of every friend to the Revolution, and of every lover of good government.

TO DAVID STUART

New York, March 28, 1790

I am sorry such jealousies as you speak of should be gaining ground, and are poisoning the minds of the southern people. . . .

That there is a diversity of interests in the Union none has denied. That this is the case also in every State is equally certain. And that it even extends to the counties of individual States can be as readily proved. Instance the southern and northern parts of Virginia, the upper and lower parts of South Carolina, etc. Have not the interests of these always been at variance? . . . These are well known truths, and yet it did not follow that separation was to result from the disagreement.

To constitute a dispute there must be two parties. To understand it well both parties and all the circumstances must be fully heard, and to accommodate differences, temper and mutual forbearance are requisite. Common danger brought the States into confederacy, and on their union our safety and importance depend. A spirit of accommodation was the basis of the present Constitution. Can it be expected then that the Southern or the Eastern part of the Empire will succeed in all their measures? Certainly not. But I will readily grant that more points will be carried by the latter than the former, and for the reason . . . that in all great national questions they move in unison whilst the others are divided. But I ask again which is most blame-worthy, those who see, and will steadily pursue their interest, or those who cannot see, or seeing will not act wisely? And I will ask another question, of the highest magnitude in my mind, to wit, if the eastern and northern States are dangerous *in Union*, will they be less so in separation? If self interest is their governing principle will it forsake them or be less restrained by such an event? I hardly think it would. Then, independent of other considerations, what would Virginia . . . gain by a separation? Would they not, most unquestionably, be the weaker party?

TO MARQUIS DE LAFAYETTE

New York, June 3, 1790

You have doubtless been informed from time to time of the happy progress of our affairs. The principal difficulties which opposed themselves in any shape to the prosperous execution of our government seem in a great measure to have been surmounted. A good temper prevails among our citizens. Rhode Island has just now acceded to the Constitution, and has thus united under the general government all the States of the original Confederacy.

. . . Our government is now happily carried into operation. Although some thorny questions still remain, it is to be hoped that the wisdom of those concerned in the national legislature will dispose of them prudently. A funding system is one of the subjects which occasions most anxiety and perplexity. Yet our revenues have been considerably more productive than it was imagined they would be. In the last year, the plentiful crops and great prices of grain, have vastly augmented our remittances. The rate of exchange is also much in our favor. Importations of European goods have been uncommonly extensive, and the duties pay-

able into the public Treasury proportionably so. Our trade to
the East Indies flourishes. The profits to individuals are so considerable as to induce more persons to engage in it.

TO DAVID STUART

New York, June 15, 1790

The question of Assumption [of state debts by the federal
government] has occupied a great deal of time, and no wonder;
for it is certainly a very important one; and, under *proper* restrictions, and scrutiny into accounts will be found, I conceive, to be
just. The cause in which the expenses of the war was incurred,
was a common cause. The States (in Congress) declared it so at
the beginning and pledged themselves to stand by each other. If
then, some States were harder pressed than others, or from particular or local circumstances contracted heavier debts, it is but
reasonable when this fact is ascertained . . . that an allowance
ought to be made them when due credit is given to others. Had
the invaded, and hard pressed States believed the case would have
been otherwise, opposition in them would very soon, I believe,
have changed to submission and given a different termination to
the war.

TO COMTE DE ROCHAMBEAU

New York, August 10, 1790

The little anecdote which you recall to mind, my dear
Count, of your countrymen at Rhode Island who burnt their
mouths with the hot soup, while mine waited leisurely for it to
cool, perhaps, when politically applied in the manner you have
done, has not less truth than pleasantry in its resemblance of national characters. But if there shall be no worse consequence resulting from too great eagerness in swallowing something so de-
lightful as liberty, than that of suffering a momentary pain or
making a ridiculous figure with a scalded mouth, upon the whole
it may be said you Frenchmen have come off well, considering how
immoderately you thirsted for the cup of liberty. And no wonder,
as you drank it to the bottom, that some licentiousness should
have been mingled with the dregs.

TO MARQUIS DE LAFAYETTE

Philadelphia, July 28, 1791

The complete establishment of our public credit is a strong mark of the confidence of the people in the virtue of their Representatives, and the wisdom of their measures; and, while in Europe, wars or commotions seem to agitate almost every nation, peace and tranquillity prevail among us, except on some parts of our western frontiers, where the Indians have been troublesome, to reclaim or chastise whom proper measures are now pursuing. This contrast between the situation of the people of the United States, and those of Europe is too striking to be passed over, even by the most superficial observer, and may, I believe, be considered as one great cause of leading the people here to reflect more attentively on their own prosperous state, and to examine more minutely, and consequently approve more fully of the government under which they live, than they otherwise would have done. But we do not wish to be the only people who may taste the sweets of an equal and good government; we look with an anxious eye to the time when happiness and tranquillity shall prevail in your country, and when all Europe shall be freed from commotions, tumults, and alarms.

TO GOVERNOR GEORGE CLINTON

Philadelphia, September 14, 1791

I feel a due concern for any injury, inconvenience or dissatisfaction which may have arisen or may arise, in respect to the State of New-York, or any part of its inhabitants, in consequence of the [British] detention of the [Northwest] posts, or the interferences which may have grown out of it. Nor has the matter failed to receive from me the degree of attention to which it is entitled. Yet in a point of such vast magnitude as that of the preservation of the peace of the Union, particularly in this still *very early* stage of our affairs, and at a period so little remote from a most exhausting and affecting, though successful war, the public welfare and safety evidently enjoin a conduct of circumspection, moderation and forbearance. And it is relied upon, that the known good sense of the community ensures its approbation of such a conduct.

There are, however, bounds to the spirit of forbearance, which ought not to be exceeded. Events may occur which may demand a departure from it. But if extremities are at any time to ensue, it is of the utmost consequence that they should be the result of a deliberate plan, not of an accidental collision; and that they should appear both at home and abroad to have flowed either from a necessity which left no alternative, or from a combination of advantageous circumstances which left no doubt of the expediency of hazarding them. Under the impression of this opinion and supposing that the event which is apprehended should be realized, it is my desire that no hostile measure be in the first instance attempted.

TO JEAN BAPTISTE TERNANT

Mount Vernon, September 24, 1791

I have not delayed a moment since the receipt of your communications, in dispatching orders to the Secretary of the Treasury to furnish the money, and to the Secretary of War to deliver the arms and ammunition, which you have applied to me for.

Sincerely regretting, as I do, the cause which has given rise to this application, I am happy in the opportunity of testifying how well disposed the United States are to render every aid in their power to our good friends and allies the French to quell "the alarming insurrection of the Negros in Hispaniola" and of the ready disposition to effect it, of the Executive authority thereof.

TO JOHN VAUGHAN

Philadelphia, December 27, 1791

Lamentable! to see such a spirit of revolt among the Blacks. Where it will stop, is difficult to say.

TO THE SECRETARY OF THE TREASURY

Mount Vernon, July 29, 1792

On my way home, and since my arrival here, I have endeavored to learn from sensible and moderate men, known friends to the government, the sentiments which are entertained of public measures. These all agree that the country is prosperous and happy; but they seem to be alarmed at that system of policy, and those interpretations of the Constitution which have taken place in Congress. Others, less friendly perhaps to the Government, and more disposed to arraign the conduct of its officers . . . go further, and enumerate a variety of matters, which as well as I can recollect, may be adduced under the following heads. Viz.

First. That the public debt is greater than we can possibly pay. . . .

4th. They cite propositions in Congress, and suspect other projects on foot, still to increase the mass of the debt. . . .

10th. That all the capital employed in paper speculation is barren and useless, producing, like that on a gaming table, no accession to itself, and is withdrawn from commerce and agriculture where it would have produced addition to the common mass.

11th. That it nourishes in our citizens vice and idleness instead of industry and morality.

12th. That it has furnished effectual means of corrupting such a portion of the legislature, as turns the balance between the honest voters whichever way it is directed.

13th. That this corrupt squadron, deciding the voice of the legislature, . . . [have] manifested their disposition to get rid of the limitations imposed by the Constitution on the general legislature; limitations, on the faith of which, the States acceded to that instrument.

14th. That the ultimate object of all this is to prepare the way for a change, from the present republican form of Government, to that of a monarchy; of which the British Constitution is to be the model.

15th. That this was contemplated in the Convention, they say is no secret, because its partisans have made none of it; to effect it then was impracticable; but they are still eager after their object, and are predisposing everything for its ultimate attainment.

16th. So many of them have got into the legislature, that, aided by the corrupt squadron of paper dealers, who are at their devotion, they make a majority in both houses. . . .

18th. Of all the mischiefs objected to the system of measures before mentioned, none they add is so afflicting, and fatal to every honest hope, as the corruption of the legislature. As it was the earliest of these measures it became the instrument for producing the rest, and will be the instrument for producing in future a

King, Lords and Commons; or whatever else those who direct it may choose. Withdrawn such a distance from the eye of their constituents, and these so dispersed as to be inaccessible to the public information, and particularly to that of the conduct of their own Representatives, they will form the worst government upon earth, if the means of their corruption be not prevented. . . .

TO THE SECRETARY OF THE TREASURY

Mount Vernon, August 26, 1792

Differences in political opinions are as unavoidable as, to a certain point, they may, perhaps, be necessary; but it is exceedingly to be regretted that subjects cannot be discussed with temper on the one hand, or decisions submitted to without having the motives which led to them improperly implicated on the other. And this regret borders on chagrin when we find that men of abilities, zealous patriots, having the same *general* objects in view, and the same upright intentions to prosecute them, will not exercise more charity in deciding on the opinions and actions of one another. When matters get to such lengths, the natural inference is, that both sides have strained the cords beyond their bearing, and, that a middle course would be found the best, until experience shall have decided on the right way; or, which is not to be expected because it is denied to mortals, there shall be some *infallible* rule by which we could *fore-judge* events.

TO THE SECRETARY OF STATE

Philadelphia, October 18, 1792

I regret, deeply regret, the differences in opinion which have arisen, and divided you and another principal officer of the Government; and wish, devoutly, there could be an accommodation of them by mutual yieldings.

A measure of this sort would produce harmony, and consequent good in our public councils; the contrary will, inevitably, introduce confusion, and serious mischiefs; and for what? because mankind cannot think alike, but would adopt different means to attain the same end. For I will frankly, and solemnly declare that, I believe the views of both of you are pure, and well meant; and that experience alone will decide with respect to the salubrity of the measures which are the subjects of dispute. Why then, when some of the best citizens in the United States, men of discernment, uniform and tried patriots, who have no sinister views to promote, but are chaste in their ways of thinking and acting are to be found, some on one side, and some on the other of the questions which have caused these agitations, should either of you be so tenacious of your opinions as to make no allowances for those of the other? . . . I have a great, a sincere esteem and regard for you both, and ardently wish that some line could be marked out by which both of you could walk.

TO DAVID HUMPHREYS

Philadelphia, March 23, 1793

If it can be esteemed a happiness to live in an age productive of great and interesting events, we of the present age are very highly favored. The rapidity of national revolutions appear no less astonishing, than their magnitude. In what they will terminate, is known only to the great ruler of events. . . .

All our late accounts from Europe hold up the expectation of a general war in that quarter. For the sake of humanity I hope such an event will not take place; but, if it should, I trust that we shall have too just a sense of our own interest to originate any cause that may involve us in it; and I ardently wish we may not be forced into it by the conduct of other nations. If we are permitted to improve without interruption the great advantages which nature and circumstances have placed within our reach, many years will not revolve before we may be ranked not only among the most respectable, but among the happiest people on this globe.

TO THE EARL OF BUCHAN

Philadelphia, April 22, 1793

I believe it is the sincere wish of the United America to have nothing to do with the political intrigues, or the squabbles of European nations; but on the contrary, to exchange commodities and live in peace and amity with all the inhabitants of the earth. And this I am persuaded they will do, if rightfully it can be done. To administer justice to, and receive it from every power with whom they are connected will, I hope, be always found the most prominent feature in the administration of this country; and I flatter myself that nothing short of imperious necessity can occasion a breach with any of them.

TO GOVERNOR HENRY LEE

Philadelphia, July 21, 1793

That there are in this, as well as in all other countries, discontented characters, I well know; as also that these characters are actuated by very different views. Some good, from an opinion that the measures of the general government are impure; some bad, and (if I might be allowed to use so harsh an expression) diabolical, inasmuch as they are not only meant to impede the measures of that Government generally, but more especially . . . to destroy the confidence which it is necessary for the people to place . . . in their public servants.

But in what will this abuse terminate? The result, as it respects myself, I care not; for I have a consolation within, that no earthly efforts can deprive me of, and that is, that neither ambitious nor interested motives have influenced my conduct. The arrows of malevolence, therefore, however barbed and well pointed, never can reach the most vulnerable part of me; though, whilst I am *up* as a *mark*, they will be continually aimed.

TO RICHARD HENRY LEE

Mount Vernon, October 24, 1793

On fair ground, it would be difficult to assign reasons for the conduct of those who are arraigning and constantly (as far as they are able) embarrassing the measures of government with respect to its pacific disposition towards the belligerent powers in the convulsive dispute, which agitated them; but their motives are too obvious to those who have the means of information, and have viewed the different grounds they have taken, to mistake their object. It is not the cause of France (nor, I believe. of liberty) which they regard; for, could they involve this country in war (no matter with whom) and disgrace, they would be among the first and loudest of the clamorers against the expense and impolicy of the measure.

TO THOMAS JEFFERSON

Philadelphia, January 1, 1794

Since it has been impossible to prevail upon you, to forego any longer the indulgence of your desire for private life; the event, however anxious I am to avert it, must be submitted to.

But I cannot suffer you to leave your station, without assuring you, that the opinion which I had formed of your integrity and talents, and which dictated your original nomination, has been confirmed by the fullest experience; and that both have been eminently displayed in the discharge of your duties.

TO JAMES MONROE

Philadelphia, April 9, 1794

I request, if you are possessed of any facts or information, which would disqualify Colonel Hamilton for the mission to which you refer, that you would be so obliging as to communicate them to me in writing. I pledge myself, that they shall meet the most deliberate, impartial and candid consideration I am able to give them.

Colonel Hamilton and others have been mentioned, and have occurred to me as an Envoy for endeavoring by negotiation to avert the horrors of war. No one (if the measure should be adopted) is yet absolutely decided on in my mind; but . . . much will depend, among other things, upon the abilities of the person sent, and his knowledge of the affairs of this country.

TO GOUVERNEUR MORRIS

Mount Vernon, June 25, 1794

My primary objects, and to which I have steadily adhered, have been to preserve the country in peace if I can, and to be prepared for war if I cannot. To effect the first upon terms consistent with the respect which is due to ourselves, and with honor, justice and good faith to all the world, Mr. Jay (and not Mr. Jefferson as hath been suggested to you) embarked as Envoy extraordinary for England, about the middle of May. If he succeeds, well. If he does not, why, knowing the worst, we must take measures accordingly.

PROCLAMATION

Philadelphia, August 7, 1794

Whereas combinations to defeat the execution of the laws laying duties upon spirits distilled within the United States, and upon stills, have from the time of the commencement of those laws existed in some of the western parts of Pennsylvania:

And whereas the said combinations, proceeding in a manner subversive equally of the just authority of Government and of the rights of individuals, have hitherto effected their dangerous and criminal purpose; by the influence of certain irregular meetings, whose proceedings have tended to encourage and uphold the spirit of opposition; by misrepresentations of the laws calculated to render them odious; by endeavors to deter those, who might be so disposed from accepting offices under them, through fear of public resentment and of injury to person and property, and to compel those who had accepted such offices, by actual violence to surrender or forbear the execution of them; by circulating vindictive menaces against all those who should otherwise directly or indirectly aid in the execution of the said laws, or who, yielding to the dictates of conscience, and to a sense of obligation, should themselves comply therewith; by actually injuring and destroying the property of persons who were understood to have so complied; by inciting cruel and humiliating punishments upon private citizens for no other cause, than that of appearing to be friends of the laws; by intercepting the public officers on the highways, abusing, assaulting, and otherwise ill-treating them; by going to their houses in the night, gaining admittance by force, taking away their papers, and committing other outrages, employing for these unwarrantable purposes the agency of armed banditti disguised in such manner as for the most part to escape discovery:

And whereas the endeavors of the Legislature to obviate objections to the said laws, by lowering the duties and by other alterations conducive to the convenience of those whom they immediately affect (though they have given satisfaction in other quarters), and the endeavors of the executive officers to conciliate a compliance with the laws, by explanations, by forbearance, and even by particular accommodations, founded on the suggestions of local considerations, have been disappointed of their effect by the machinations of persons whose industry to excite resistance has increased with every appearance of a disposition among the people to relax in their opposition and to acquiesce in the laws, insomuch that many persons in the said western parts of Pennsylvania have at length been hardy enough to perpetrate acts which I am advised amount to treason, being overt acts of levying war against the United States. . . .

Wherefore, and in pursuance of the proviso above recited, I, GEORGE WASHINGTON, President of the United States, do hereby command all persons, being insurgents as aforesaid, and all others whom it may concern, on or before the first day of September next, to disperse and retire peaceably to their respective abodes. And I do moreover warn all persons whomsoever against aiding, abetting, or comforting the perpetrators of the aforesaid treasonable acts; and do require all officers and other citizens, according to their respective duties and the laws of the land, to exert their utmost endeavors to prevent and suppress such dangerous proceedings.

TO BURGES BALL

Germantown, August 10, 1794

What (under the rose I ask it) is said, or thought, as far as it has appeared to you, of the conduct of the people in the western counties of this State (Pennsylvania) towards the excise officers? And does there seem to be a disposition among those with whom you converse, to bring them to a sense of their duty, and obedience to law, by coercion, if, after they are fully notified by the Proclamation and other expedients, of the consequences of such outrageous proceedings, they do not submit to the laws of the United States, and suffer the collection of the duties upon spiritous liquors, and stills, to be made as in other places? In a word, would there be any difficulty, as far as the matter has passed under your observation, in drawing out a part of the militia of Loudoun, Berkeley and Frederick to quell this rebellious spirit, and to support order and good government?

TO GOVERNOR HENRY LEE

Germantown, August 26, 1794

I consider this insurrection as the first *formidable* fruit of the Democratic Societies; brought forth I believe too prematurely for their own views, which may contribute to the annihilation of them.

That these societies were instituted by the *artful* and *designing* members (many of their body I have no doubt mean well, but know little of the real plan), primarily to sow the seeds of jealousy and distrust among the people, of the government, by destroying all confidence in the administration of it; and that these doctrines have been budding and blowing ever since, is not new to anyone who is acquainted with the characters of their leaders, and has been attentive to their maneuvers. I early gave it as my opinion to the confidential characters around me, that, if these Societies were not counteracted (not by prosecutions, the ready way to make them grow stronger) or did not fall into disesteem from the knowledge of their origin, and the views with which they had been instituted by their father, Genêt, for purposes well known to the Government, that they would shake the government to its foundation. Time and circumstances have confirmed me in this opinion, and I deeply regret the probable consequences, not as they will affect me personally (for I have not long to act on this theatre, and sure I am that not a man amongst them can be more anxious to put me aside, than I am to sink into the profoundest retirement), but because I see, under a display of popular and fascinating guises, the most diabolical attempts to destroy the best fabric of human government and happiness that has ever been presented for the acceptance of mankind.

TO JOHN JAY

Philadelphia, August 30, 1794

I will undertake, without the gift of prophecy, to predict, that it will be impossible to keep this country in a state of amity with Great Britain long if the posts are not surrendered. A knowledge of these being *my* sentiments would have little weight I am persuaded with the British administration nor perhaps with the [British] nation, in effecting the measure. But both may rest satisfied that if they want to be in peace with this country, and to enjoy the benefits of its trade etc., to give up the posts is the only road to it. Withholding them, and the consequences we feel at present, continuing, war will be inevitable.

TO THE SECRETARY OF STATE

Fort Cumberland, October 16, 1794

I believe the eyes of all the *well* disposed people of this country will soon be opened, and that they will clearly see, the tendency if not the design of the leaders of these self created [Democratic] societies. As far as I have heard them spoken of, it is with strong reprobation. I should be extremely sorry therefore if Mr. Madison *from any cause whatsoever* should get entangled with them, or their politics.

TO JOHN JAY

Philadelphia, December 18, 1794

As I expected, and as you were informed the result would probably be, so it has happened; the western insurrection has terminated highly honorable for this country; which by the energy of its laws and the good disposition of its citizens have brought the rioters to a *perfect* sense of their misconduct without spilling a drop of blood. In the eyes of foreigners among us, this affair stands in a high point of view.

TO THE SECRETARY OF STATE

Mount Vernon, July 22, 1795

My opinion respecting the [Jay] treaty is the same now that it was: namely, not favorable to it, but that it is better to ratify it in the manner the Senate have advised . . . than to suffer matters to remain as they are, unsettled. I find endeavors are not wanting to place it in all the odious points of view, of which it is susceptible; and in some which it will not admit.

TO THE SECRETARY OF STATE

Mount Vernon, July 29, 1795

I view the opposition which the treaty is receiving from the meetings in different parts of the Union in a very serious light. Not because there is *more* weight in *any* of the objections which are made to it, than were foreseen at first; for there are *none* in *some* of them; and *gross* misrepresentations in *others*. Nor as it respects myself personally, for this shall have no influence on my conduct; plainly perceiving, and I am accordingly preparing my mind for, the obloquy which disappointment and malice are collecting to heap upon my character. But I am alarmed on account of the effect it may have on, and the advantage the French government may be disposed to make of, the spirit which is at work: to cherish a belief in them, that the treaty is calculated to favor Great Britain at their expense. Whether they believe, or disbelieve these tales, the effect . . . will be nearly the same; for whilst they are at war with that power, or so long as the animosity between the two nations exists, it will, no matter at whose expense, be their policy and it is feared it will be their conduct, to prevent us from being on good terms with Great Britain. . . . To what length this policy and interest may carry them, is problematical; but when they see the people of this country divided, and such a violent opposition given to the measures of their own government, pretend[ed]ly in their favor, it may be extremely embarrassing, to say no more of it.

To sum the whole up in a few words, I have never, since I have been in the administration of the government, seen a crisis which, in my judgment, has been so pregnant of interesting events; nor one from which more is to be apprehended.

TO ALEXANDER HAMILTON

Mount Vernon, July 29, 1795

That [the Jay treaty] has received the most tortured interpretation, and that the writings against it (which are very industriously circulated) are pregnant of the most abominable misrepresentations, admits of no doubt; yet, there are to be found, so far as my information extends, many well disposed men who conceive that in the settlement of *old* disputes, a proper regard to reciprocal justice does not appear in the treaty; whilst others, also well enough affected to the government, are of opinion that to have had *no* commercial treaty would have been better for this country, than the restricted one agreed to; inasmuch, say they, the nature of our exports and imports . . . would have forced or led to a more adequate intercourse between the two nations without any of those shackles which the treaty has imposed. In a word, that as our *exports* consists chiefly of *provisions* and *raw mate-*

rials, which to the manufacturers in Great Britain, and to their islands in the West Indies, affords employment and food, they must have had them on *our* terms, if they were not to be obtained on their *own;* whilst the *imports* of this country offers the best mart for their fabrics; and, of course, is the principal support of their manufacturers. But the string which is most played on, because it strikes with most force the popular ear, is the violation, as they term it, of our engagements with France; or in other words, the predilection shown by that instrument to Great Britain at the expense of the French nation.

TO HENRY KNOX

Mount Vernon, September 20, 1795

If any power on earth could, or the great power above would, erect the standard of infallibility in political opinions, there is no being that inhabits this terrestrial globe that would resort to it with more eagerness than myself, so long as I remain a servant of the public. But as I have found no better guide hitherto than upright intentions, and close investigation, I shall adhere to these maxims while I keep the watch; leaving it to those who will come after me to explore new ways, if they like; or think them better.

The temper of the people of this state, particularly the southern parts of it, or South Carolina and Georgia, as far as it is discoverable from the several meetings and resolutions which have been published, is adverse to the treaty with Great Britain; and yet, I doubt much whether the great body of yeomanry have formed an opinion on the subject; and whether, if their sense could be fairly taken under a plain and simple statement of facts, nine tenths of them would not advocate the measure. But with such abominable misrepresentations as appear in most of the proceedings, is it to be wondered at that uninformed minds should be affrighted with the dreadful consequences which are predicted, and are taught to expect, from the ratification of such a diabolical instrument, as the treaty is denominated.

TO PATRICK HENRY

Mount Vernon, October 9, 1795

My ardent desire is, and my aim has been to comply strictly with *all* our engagements foreign and domestic; but to keep the

United States free from *political* connections with every other country. To see that they *may be* independent of *all,* and under the influence of *none.* In a word, I want an *American* character, that the powers of Europe may be convinced we act for *ourselves* and not for *others;* this in my judgment, is the only way to be respected abroad and happy at home and not by becoming the partisans of Great Britain or France, create dissensions, disturb the public tranquillity, and destroy, perhaps for ever the cement which binds the Union.

REPLY TO THE FRENCH MINISTER

United States, January 1, 1796

Born Sir, in a land of liberty; having early learned its value; having engaged in a perilous conflict to defend it; having, in a word, devoted the best years of my life to secure its permanent establishment in my own country; my anxious recollections, my sympathetic feelings, and my best wishes are irresistibly excited, whensoever, in any country, I see an oppressed nation unfurl the banners of freedom. But above all, the events of the French Revolution have produced the deepest solicitude, as well as the highest admiration. To call your nation brave, were to pronounce but common praise. Wonderful people! Ages to come will read with astonishment the history of your brilliant exploits! I rejoice that the interesting revolutionary movements of so many years have issued in the formation of a constitution designed to give permanency to the great object for which you have contended. I rejoice that liberty, which you have so long embraced with enthusiasm, liberty, of which you have been the invincible defenders, now finds an asylum in the bosom of a regularly organized government; a government, which, being formed to secure the happiness of the French people, corresponds with the ardent wishes of my heart, while it gratifies the pride of every citizen of the United States by its resemblance to their own. On these glorious events, accept, Sir, my sincere congratulations.

In delivering to you these sentiments, I express not my own feelings only, but those of my fellow citizens in relation to the commencement, the progress, and the issue of the French revolution. And they will cordially join with me in purest wishes to the Supreme Being, that the citizens of our sister republic, our magnanimous allies, may soon enjoy in peace that liberty which they have purchased at so great a price, and all the happiness which liberty can bestow.

TO GOVERNOR JOHN JAY

Philadelphia, May 8, 1796

I am *sure* the mass of Citizens in these United States *mean well*, and I firmly believe they will always *act well*, whenever they can obtain a right understanding of matters; but in some parts of the Union, where the sentiments of their delegates and leaders are adverse to the government and great pains are taken to inculcate a belief that their rights are assailed, and their liberties endangered, it is not easy to accomplish this; especially, as is the case invariably, when the inventors and abetters of pernicious measures use infinitely more industry in disseminating the poison, than the well disposed part of the community to furnish the antidote. To this source all our discontents may be traced and from it our embarrassments proceed. Hence serious misfortunes originating in misrepresentation frequently flow and spread before they can be dissipated by truth.

TO THOMAS JEFFERSON

Mount Vernon, July 6, 1796

As you have mentioned the subject yourself, it would not be frank, candid, or friendly to conceal, that your conduct has been represented as derogatory from that opinion I had conceived you entertained of me. That to your particular friends and connections you have described, and they have denounced me, as a person under a dangerous influence [of Alexander Hamilton]; and that, if I would listen *more* to some *other* opinions, all would be well. My answer invariably has been, that I had never discovered anything in the conduct of Mr. Jefferson to raise suspicions, in my mind, of his insincerity; that if he would retrace my public conduct while he was in the administration, abundant proofs would occur to him, that truth and right decisions were the *sole* object of my pursuit; that there were as many instances within his *own* knowledge of my having decided *against,* as in *favor of* the opinions of the person evidently alluded to; and moreover, that I was no believer in the infallibility of the politics or measures of *any man living*. In short, that I was no party man myself, and the first wish of my heart was, if parties did exist, to reconcile them.

To this I may add, and very truly, that, until within the last year or two ago, I had no conception that parties would or even could go the length I have been witness to; nor did I believe until lately, that it was within the bounds of probability; hardly within those of possibility, that, while I was using my utmost exertions to establish a national character of our own, independent, as far as our obligations and justice would permit, of every nation of the earth; and wished, by steering a steady course, to preserve this country from the horrors of a desolating war, that I should be accused of being the enemy of one nation, and subject to the influence of another; and to prove it, that every act of my administration would be tortured, and the grossest and most insidious misrepresentations of them be made. But enough of this; I have already gone farther in the expression of my feelings than I intended.

FAREWELL ADDRESS

United States, September 19, 1796

The basis of our political systems is the right of the people to make and to alter their Constitutions of Government. But the Constitution which at any time exists, 'till changed by an explicit and authentic act of the whole people, is sacredly obligatory upon all. The very idea of the power and the right of the people to establish Government presupposes the duty of every individual to obey the established Government.

All obstructions to the execution of the laws, all combinations and associations, under whatever plausible character, with the real design to direct, control, counteract, or awe the regular deliberation and action of the constituted authorities are destructive of this fundamental principle and of fatal tendency. They serve to organize faction, to give it an artificial and extraordinary force; to put in the place of the delegated will of the nation, the will of a party; often a small but artful and enterprising minority of the community; and, according to the alternate triumphs of different parties, to make the public administration the mirror of the ill concerted and incongruous projects of faction, rather than the organ of consistent and wholesome plans digested by common councils and modified by mutual interests. However combinations or associations of the above description may now and then answer popular ends, they are likely, in the course of time and things, to become potent engines, by which cunning, ambitious and unprincipled men will be enabled to subvert the power of the people, and to usurp for themselves the reins of Government; destroying afterwards the very engines which have lifted them to unjust dominion.

Towards the preservation of your Government and the permanency of your present happy state, it is requisite, not only that you steadily discountenance irregular oppositions to its acknowledged authority, but also that you resist with care the spirit of innovation upon its principles however specious the pretexts. One method of assault may be to effect, in the forms of the Constitution, alterations which will impair the energy of the system, and thus to undermine what cannot be directly overthrown. In all the changes to which you may be invited, remember that time and habit are at least as necessary to fix the true character of Governments, as of other human institutions; that experience is the surest standard by which to test the real tendency of the existing Constitution of a country; that facility in changes upon the credit of mere hypotheses and opinion exposes to perpetual change, from the endless variety of hypotheses and opinion; and remember, especially, that for the efficient management of your common interests, in a country so extensive as ours, a Government of as much vigor as is consistent with the perfect security of liberty is indispensable. . . .

I have already intimated to you the danger of parties in the state, with particular reference to the founding of them on geographical discriminations. Let me now take a more comprehensive view, and warn you in the most solemn manner against the baneful effects of the spirit of party, generally:

This spirit, unfortunately, is inseparable from our nature, having its root in the strongest passions of the human mind. It exists under different shapes in all Governments, more or less stifled, controlled, or repressed; but, in those of the popular form it is seen in its greatest rankness and is truly their worst enemy.

The alternate domination of one faction over another, sharpened by the spirit of revenge natural to party dissension, which in different ages and countries has perpetrated the most horrid enormities, is itself a frightful despotism. But this leads at length to a more formal and permanent despotism. The disorders and miseries which result, gradually incline the minds of men to seek security and repose in the absolute power of an individual; and sooner or later the chief of some prevailing faction more able or more fortunate than his competitors, turns this disposition to the purposes of his own elevation, on the ruins of public liberty. . . .

So likewise, a passionate attachment of one nation for another produces a variety of evils. Sympathy for the favorite nation, facilitating the illusion of an imaginary common interest, in cases where no real common interest exists, and infusing into one the enmities of the other, betrays the former into a participation in the quarrels and wars of the latter, without adequate inducement or justification. It leads also to concessions to the favorite nation of privileges denied to others, which is apt doubly to injure the nation making the concessions; by unnecessarily parting with what ought to have been retained; and by exciting jealousy, ill will, and a disposition to retaliate, in the parties from whom equal privileges are withheld. And it gives to ambitious, corrupted, or deluded citizens (who devote themselves to the favorite nation) facility to betray, or sacrifice the interests of their own country, without odium, sometimes even with popularity; gilding with the appearances of a virtuous sense of obligation a commendable deference for public opinion, or a laudable zeal for public good, the base or foolish compliances of ambition, corruption or infatuation. . . .

Against the insidious wiles of foreign influence (I conjure you to believe me fellow citizens), the jealousy of a free people ought to be *constantly* awake; since history and experience prove that foreign influence is one of the most baneful foes of Republican Government. But that jealousy to be useful must be impartial; else it becomes the instrument of the very influence to be avoided, instead of a defence against it. Excessive partiality for one foreign nation and excessive dislike of another, cause those whom they actuate to see danger only on one side, and serve to veil and even second the arts of influence on the other. Real patriots, who may resist the intrigues of the favorite, are liable to become suspected and odious; while its tools and dupes usurp the applause and confidence of the people, to surrender their interests.

The great rule of conduct for us, in regard to foreign nations is in extending our commercial relations to have with them as little *political* connection as possible. So far as we have already formed engagements let them be fulfilled, with perfect good faith. Here let us stop.

TO THE CITIZENS OF ALEXANDRIA
AND ITS NEIGHBORHOOD

March 23, 1797

Having obeyed the calls of my country, and spent the prime of my life in rendering it the best services of which my abilities were capable; and finding that the infirmities of age were creeping upon me, it became as necessary, as it was congenial to my feelings, to seek, in the shades of retirement, the repose I had always contemplated.

To have finished my public career to the satisfaction of my fellow-citizens, will, to my latest moments, be matter of pleasing reflection; and to find an evidence of this approbation among my neighbors and friends (some of whom have been the companions of my juvenile years) will contribute not a little to heighten the enjoyment.

No wish in my retirement can exceed that of seeing our country happy; and I can entertain no doubt of its being so, if all of us act the part of good citizens; contributing our best endeavors to maintain the Constitution, support the laws, and guard our independence against all assaults from whatsoever quarter they may come. Clouds may and doubtless often will, in the vicissitudes of events, hover over our political concerns, but a steady adherence to these principles will not only dispel them but render our prospects the brighter by such temporary obscurities.

For the affectionate and flattering manner in which you have been pleased to express your regrets on the occasion of my relinquishing public employment, and for your congratulations on my return to my long forsaken residence at Mt. Vernon, I pray you to accept my warmest acknowledgments, and the assurances of the additional pleasure I shall derive from the prospect of spending the remainder of my days in ease and tranquillity among you; employed in rural pursuits, and in the exercise of domestic and other duties.

PART TWO

THE WORLD LOOKS AT WASHINGTON

The following fifty documents relating to Washington span a period of sixty years, from the Indian Half King's peevish account in 1754 to Thomas Jefferson's balanced summary in 1814. Here are contained the rather obvious reasons most Americans admired Washington: his patriotism, his perseverance, his considerable self-sacrifice, his incorruptibility. Here, also, are the reasons other Americans dissented: his overly cautious military command, his intellectual mediocrity, his aristocratic demeanor, his possession of slaves, his endorsement of the Constitution which antifederalists distrusted, his repressive measures during the Whiskey Rebellion, his approval of Jay's treaty. The fact that a democratic nation could so exalt and venerate Washington was a matter of deep concern to the dissenters. In short, Washington was a controversial figure. To most Americans he was indispensable. To others he was a fallible human who should have died before he could become President, when—they believed—he virtually allied America to Britain against France, became increasingly authoritarian, and was little more than a popular idol used by the Federalists for partisan purposes.

JOURNAL OF CONRAD WEISER [1]

September 3, 1754

By the way, Tanacharisson, otherwise called the Half King, complained very much of the behavior of Col. Washington to him (though in a very moderate way, saying the Colonel was a good-natured man but had no experience), saying that he took upon him to command the Indians as his slaves, and would have them

[1] "Journal of the Proceedings of Conrad Weiser . . . ," in *Minutes of the Provincial Council of Pennsylvania* (Harrisburg, 1851), VI, 151–52.

every day upon the out Scout and attack the enemy by themselves, and that he would by no means take advice from the Indians; that he lay at one place from one full Moon to the other and made no fortifications at all, but that little thing upon the meadow, where he thought the French would come up to him in open field; that had he taken the Half King's advice and made such fortifications as the Half King advised him to make he would certainly have beat the French off. . . . The French had acted as great cowards and the English as fools in that engagement. . . . Col. Washington would never listen to them, but was always driving them on to fight by his directions.

NATHANIEL GIST TO GEORGE WASHINGTON [2]

October 15, 1755

Your name is more talked of in Pennsylvania than that of any other person in the army, and everybody seems willing to venture under your command. If you would send some discreet person, I doubt not he would enlist a good number. . . .

WILLIAM FAIRFAX TO GEORGE WASHINGTON [3]

April, 1756

Your endeavors in the service and defence of your country must redound to your honor; therefore do not let any unavoidable interruptions sicken your mind in the attempts you may pursue. Your good health and fortune are the toast at every table. Among the Romans, such a general acclamation and public regard, shown to any of their chieftains, were always esteemed a high honor, and gratefully accepted.

CONSTITUTIONAL GAZETTE [4]

August 23, 1775

Last Sabbath, a child of Colonel Robinson of Dorchester, Massachusetts, was baptized . . . by the name of GEORGE WASHINGTON.

[2] Jared Sparks, ed., *The Writings of George Washington* (New York, 1847), II, 109 fn.

[3] *Ibid.*, II, 145 fn.

[4] Frank Moore, ed., *Diary of the American Revolution* (New York, 1858), I, 121.

BENJAMIN RUSH TO THOMAS RUSHTON [5]

October 29, 1775

General Washington has astonished his most intimate friends with a display of the most wonderful talents for the government of an army. His zeal, his disinterestedness, his activity, his politeness, and his manly behavior to General Gage in their late correspondence have captivated the hearts of the public and his friends. He seems to be one of those illustrious heroes whom providence raises up once in three or four hundred years to save a nation from ruin. If you do not know his person, perhaps you will be pleased to hear that he has so much martial dignity in his deportment that you would distinguish him to be a general and a soldier from among ten thousand people. There is not a king in Europe that would not look like a valet de chambre by his side.

ADDRESS OF THE MASSACHUSETTS COUNCIL AND HOUSE OF REPRESENTATIVES TO GEORGE WASHINGTON [6]

March 29, 1776

May it please Your Excellency:

When the liberties of America were attacked by the violent hand of oppression; when troops, hostile to the rights of humanity, invaded this colony, seized our capital, and spread havoc and destruction around it; when our virtuous sons were murdered, and our houses destroyed by the troops of Britain, the inhabitants of this and the other American colonies, impelled by self-preservation and the love of freedom, forgetting their domestic concerns, determined resolutely and unitedly to oppose the sons of tyranny.

Convinced of the vast importance of having a gentleman of great military accomplishments to discipline, lead, and conduct the forces of the colonies, it gave us the greatest satisfaction to hear that the honorable congress of the united colonies had made

[5] L. H. Butterfield, ed., *Letters of Benjamin Rush,* 2 Vols. (Philadelphia: The American Philosophical Society [*Memoirs of the American Philosophical Society,* Vol. 30]; Princeton: Princeton University Press, 1951), I, 92. Copyright 1951 by The American Philosophical Society. The selections from this book are reprinted by permission of the publishers and the author.

[6] Hezekiah Niles, ed., *Principles and Acts of the Revolution in America* (Baltimore, 1822), pp. 143–44.

choice of a gentleman thus qualified; who, leaving the pleasure of domestic and rural life, was ready to undertake the arduous task. And your nobly declining to accept the pecuniary emoluments annexed to this high office, fully evidenced to us that a warm regard to the sacred rights of humanity, and sincere love to your country, solely influenced you in the acceptance of this important trust.

From your acknowledged abilities as a soldier, and your virtues in public and private life, we had the most pleasing hopes; but the fortitude and equanimity so conspicuous in your conduct; the wisdom of your counsels; the mild, yet strict government of the army; your attention to the civil constitution of this colony; the regard you have at all times shown for the lives and health of those under your command; the fatigues you have with cheerfulness endured; the regard you have shown for the preservation of our metropolis, and the great address with which our military operations have been conducted, have exceeded our most sanguine expectations, and demand the warmest returns of gratitude. . . .

May you still go on approved by Heaven, revered by all good men, and dreaded by those tyrants who claim their fellow men as their property. May the united colonies be defended from slavery by your victorious arms. May they still see their enemies flying before you; and (the deliverance of your country being effected) may you, in retirement, enjoy that peace and satisfaction of mind, which always attends the good and great. And may future generations in the peaceful enjoyment of that freedom, the exercise of which your sword shall establish, raise the richest and most lasting monuments to the name of a *Washington*.

JOURNAL OF AMBROSE SERLE [7]

July 16, 1776

Another flag of truce was sent today with a letter to Washington from the General [Howe], which was refused for the same idle and insolent reasons as were given before. Their leaders seem determined to risk everything, rather than abate of their new power and consequence; so that blows and war seem inevitable. There is this reflection on our side, that we strove as far as decency

[7] Edward H. Tatum, ed., *The American Journal of Ambrose Serle: Secretary to Lord Howe, 1776–1778* (San Marino: The Huntington Library, 1940), pp. 35–36. Reprinted by permission of The Huntington Library.

and honor could permit, or humanity itself demand, to avert all bloodshed and to promote an accommodation. And yet, it seems to be beneath a little paltry Colonel of Militia [Washington], at the head of a Banditti or Rebels, to treat with the Representative of His lawful Sovereign, because 'tis impossible for . . . [Howe] to give all the titles which the poor creature requires. Rebellion is indeed as the sin of witchcraft, blinds the eyes, and hardens the heart against every sound principle of religion and duty. If such men in such a cause can prosper, it is only the prosperity of a night, which the morning cloud shall chase away.

JOSEPH REED, ADJUTANT GENERAL, TO MAJOR-GENERAL CHARLES LEE [8]

November 21, 1776

. . . General Washington's own judgment, seconded by representations from us, would, I believe, have saved the men and their arms; but unluckily, General Greene's judgment was contrary. This kept the General's mind in a state of suspense till the stroke was struck. Oh, General! An indecisive mind is one of the greatest misfortunes that can befall an army. How often have I lamented it this campaign!

MAJOR-GENERAL CHARLES LEE TO JOSEPH REED [9]

November 24, 1776

I received your most obliging, flattering letter; lament with you that fatal indecision of mind which in war is a much greater disqualification than stupidity or even want of personal courage. Accident may put a decisive blunderer in the right, but eternal defeat and miscarriage must attend the man of the best parts if cursed with indecision.

PENNSYLVANIA JOURNAL[10]

February 19, 1777

Who is the best man living? His Excellency General Washington, to whom the title of Excellency is applied with the great-

[8] *A Reprint of the Reed and Cadwalader Pamphlets with an Appendix* (n.p., 1863), Appendix D.

[9] *Ibid.,* Appendix E.

[10] Moore, ed., *Diary of the American Revolution,* I, 396–97.

est propriety. He has left a peaceful habitation and an affluent fortune to encounter all the dangers and hardships of war, nobly stepping forth in the defense of truth, justice, and his country. In private life he wins the hearts and wears the love of all who are so happy as to live within the sphere of his action. In his public character he commands universal respect and admiration. Conscious that the principles on which he acts are indeed founded on virtue, he steadily and cooly pursues those principles, with a mind neither depressed by disappointments nor elated by success, giving full exercise to that discretion and wisdom which he so eminently possesses. He retreats like a general and acts like a hero. If there are spots in his character, they are like the spots in the sun, only discernible by the magnifying powers of a telescope. Had he lived in the days of idolatry, he had been worshipped as a god. One age cannot do justice to his merit, but the united voices of a grateful posterity shall pay a cheering tribute of undissembled praise to the great asserter of their country's freedom.

REMARK OF JOHN ADAMS TO THE CONTINENTAL CONGRESS [11]

February 19, 1777

I have been distressed to see some members of this house disposed to idolise an image which their own hands have molten. I speak here of the superstitious veneration that is sometimes paid to General Washington. Altho' I honor him for his good qualities, yet in this house I feel myself his superior. In private life I shall always acknowledge that he is mine.

REVEREND JACOB DUCHÉ TO GEORGE WASHINGTON [12]

October 8, 1777

Dear Sir, suffer me, in the language of truth and real affection, to address myself to you. All the world must be convinced you are engaged in the service of your country from motives perfectly disinterested. You risked everything that was dear to you,

[11] Edmund C. Burnett, ed., *Letters of Members of the Continental Congress* (Washington, D.C.: Carnegie Institute of Washington, 1923), II, 263. The selections from this book are reprinted by permission of the publisher.

[12] Jared Sparks, ed., *Correspondence of the American Revolution; Being Letters of Eminent Men to George Washington* (Boston, 1853), I, 451–57.

abandoned the sweets of domestic life, which your affluent fortune can give the uninterrupted enjoyment of. But had you, could you have had, the least idea of matters being carried to such a dangerous extremity? Your most intimate friends shuddered at the thought of a separation from the mother country, and I took it for granted that your sentiments coincided with theirs. What, then, can be the consequence of this rash and violent measure, and degeneracy of representation, confusion of councils, blunders without number? The most respectable characters have withdrawn themselves, and are succeeded by a great majority of illiberal and violent men. Take an impartial view of the present Congress, and what can you expect from them? Your feelings must be greatly hurt by the representation of your native province. . . . From the New England provinces can you find one that, as a gentleman, you could wish to associate with? . . . Are the dregs of Congress, then, still to influence a mind like yours? These are not the men you engaged to serve; these are not the men that America has chosen to represent her. Most of them were chosen by a little, low faction, and the few gentlemen that are among them now are well known to lie on the balance, and looking up to your hand alone to turn the beam. 'Tis you, Sir, and you only, that support the present Congress; of this you must be fully sensible. Long before they left Philadelphia, their dignity and consequence were gone. . . .

After this view of the Congress, turn to the army. The whole world knows that its only existence depends upon you; that your death or captivity disperses it in a moment, and that there is not a man on that [revolutionary] side [of] the question, in America, capable of succeeding you. As to the army itself, what have you to expect from them? Have they not frequently abandoned you yourself, in the hour of extremity? Can you have the least confidence in a set of undisciplined men and officers, many of whom have been taken from the lowest of people, without principle, without courage? Take away them that surround your person, how very few are there that you can ask to sit at your table! As to your little navy, of that little, what is left? . . .

And now, where are your resources? Oh! My dear Sir, how sadly have you been abused by a faction devoid of truth, and void of tenderness to you and your country! They have amused you with hopes of a declaration of war on the part of France. Believe me, from the best authority, it was a fiction from the first. . . . From your friends in England you have nothing to expect. Their numbers have diminished to a cipher; the spirit of the whole nation is in activity; a few sounding names among the nobility, though perpetually ringing in your ears, are without character, without influence. Disappointed ambition has made them desperate, and they only wish to make the deluded Americans instruments of revenge. All orders and ranks of men in Great Britain are now unanimous, and determined to risk their all with content. . . .

In America, your harbors are blocked up, your cities fall one after another; fortress after fortress, battle after battle is lost. A British army, after having passed unmolested through a vast extent of country, have possessed themselves of the capital of America. How unequal the contest! How fruitless the expense of blood! Under so many discouraging circumstances, can virtue, can honor, can the love of your country, prompt you to proceed? Humanity itself, and surely humanity is no stranger to your breast, calls upon you to desist. Your army must perish for want of common necessaries, or thousands of innocent families must perish to support them; wherever they encamp, the country must be impoverished; wherever they march, the troops of Britain will pursue, and must complete the destruction which America herself has begun. Perhaps it may be said, it is better to die than to be made slaves. This, indeed, is a splendid maxim in theory, and perhaps, in some instances, may be found experimentally true; but when there is the least probability of a happy accommodation, surely wisdom and humanity call for some sacrifices to be made, to prevent inevitable destruction. . . .

It is to you, and you alone, your bleeding country looks, and calls aloud for this sacrifice. . . . May Heaven inspire you with this glorious resolution of exerting your strength, at this crisis, and immortalizing yourself as friend and guardian to your country! Your penetrating eye needs not more explicit language to discern my meaning. With that prudence and delicacy, therefore, of which I know you possess, represent to Congress the indispensable necessity of rescinding the hasty and ill-advised declaration of independency. . . .

Oh! Sir, let no false ideas of worldly honor deter you from engaging in so glorious a task. Whatever censure may be thrown out by mean, illiberal minds, your character will rise in the estimation of the virtuous and noble. It will appear with lustre in the annals of history, and form a glorious contrast to that of those who have fought to obtain conquest, and gratify their own ambition by the destruction of their species and the ruin of their country.

RIVINGTON'S GAZETTE [13]

January 3, 1778

At Edmonton, in England, a gibbet was erected, under which a load of wood was laid, and from the gibbet was hung a figure, with a mask for a face, and on its breast a label, with this inscription: "Washington, General of the Americans." And in the evening the gibbet, and the general, were reduced to ashes.

HENRY LAURENS TO ISAAC MOTTE [14]

January 26, 1778

We have been from time to time for above a month past alarmed by accounts from the Commander in Chief of the near and almost inevitable dispersion of the Army from a want of provision. Nakedness is cheerfully submitted to. The General has made the most affecting complaints of neglect in the principal departments, has proceeded even to say that "never was Officer so impeded as he has been." Yet, I intimate it with deep feeling and much regret, too little regard has been paid to his sensible, spirited, manly representations. This great and virtuous man has not acted the *half patriot,* by a hasty resignation. His complaints are well founded. . . . No internal enemy can hurt him without his own consent. I trust he will not gratify the wishes of those who seek to remove him, if there be any such.

LUND WASHINGTON TO GEORGE WASHINGTON [15]

February 18, 1778

Colonel Mason . . . tells me he was informed of the cabal against you, before he left Williamsburg, and some had hinted to him that R. H. Lee was one suspected of having a hand in it, and as they knew the intimacy existing between them, begged that he would talk to Lee and discover whether anything of the sort

[13] Moore, ed., *Diary of the American Revolution,* I, 519.

[14] Burnett, ed., *Letters,* III, 51–52.

[15] Kate Mason Rowland, *The Life of George Mason, 1725–1792* (New York, 1892), II, 474–75.

was in agitation or not. He did so. That Lee declares no such thing or even a hint has ever been mentioned in Congress, and that he should look upon it as one of the greatest misfortunes that could befall this continent, should you by any means whatever give up the command of the army, for fully convinced he was in his own opinion no other man upon this continent was equal to the task; that he had often lamented the heavy burden you bear, and the difficulties you had to surmount more than any man ever had before. For his part he looked upon it as one among the many favors we had received from above, that the Supreme Being had been pleased to save and protect in the most miraculous degree the only man in whom every one could confide in. Mr. Mason is of opinion it is a Tory maneuver for he thinks no friend to America can be an enemy to you, for "by ———," which was his expression, there is not nor ever was in the world a man who acted from a more laudable and disinterested motive than you do, and that he defied all history to show a war, begun, and carried on, under more disadvantages than the present; nor, he would venture to affirm, one that had been better conducted so far as it depended on the Commander in Chief, for that he had observed you had foreseen and pointed out what would be the event of all the blunders committed by the different legislatures, and that wherever you had given your opinion the event had proved you were right, then enumerated a number of instances to prove his assertion.

THOMAS BURKE TO THE NORTH CAROLINA ASSEMBLY [16]

April 29, 1778

I have penetrated the personal character of General Washington. In my judgment he is a good officer and most excellent citizen, moved only by the most amiable and disinterested patriotism. He perseveres in encountering extreme difficulties, dangers and fatigues under which he seems sensible of no uneasiness but from the misfortunes of his country, and of no pleasure but from her success. His few defects are only the excess of his amiable qualities, and though I am not of opinion that any individual is absolutely essential to the success of our cause, yet I am persuaded his loss would be very severely felt, and would not be easily supplied.

[16] Burnett, ed., *Letters*, III, 201.

DER PENNSYLVANISCHE STAATS COURIER ODER
EINLAUFENDE WOCHENTLICHE NACHRICHTEN [17]

May 6, 1778

Conversation of two farmers in Tolpehacken, of an evening over a glass of whiskey and good hickory fire, May 1, 1778:

What news is there? What do the rebels say?
What is the base rabble, with their companions, saying?
They aren't saying very much; but their actions and
   conduct any one can immediately read from a picture
   thought up by a rogue in Lancaster.
Do tell me how the fellow made it?
He represents Washington on a throne,
What further? Go on, come whisper it in my ear.
The king lies before him on one bended knee.
Is this really so? Sir, it is no lie;
   and what is still worse, he is supposed to beckon with
   his finger for the king to bend the other knee as well.
Is not that insolent? The crime must be punished.
Is that a free people? No—they are slaves of Congress.
   Up!
Up! Up! Ye Britons, up! Ye Hessians, gather courage!
Just advance briskly. The king's cause is safe.
As long as sun and moon illumine the globe,
   the streams Delaware and Schuylkill unite,
   till the structure of the earth and firmament grow old,
   Britain's hero-hand shall keep the scepter upright.

JOURNAL OF ADJUTANT GENERAL MAJOR BAURMEISTER
OF THE HESSIAN FORCES [18]

May, 1778

On the 30th [of April] the rich and influential Quakers returned from their prisons, in which they had been confined from the time the rebels, after the action at Brandywine, were obliged

---

[17] Ray W. Pettengill, ed., *Letters from America, 1776–1779* (Port Washington, New York: Kennikat Press, 1964), p. 195. Reprinted by permission of the publisher.

[18] Bernard A. Uhlendorf, ed., *Revolution in America: Confidential Letters and Journals 1776–1784 of Adjutant General Major Baurmeister of the Hessian Forces* (New Brunswick: Rutgers University Press, 1957), pp. 167–68. The selections from this book are reprinted by permission of the publisher.

to leave this city [Philadelphia], and in which they were treated in no gentle manner. I cannot but tell your Lordship that the wives of four of these Quakers asked permission at the English headquarters to go and beg for the release of their husbands. General Washington, in camp at Valley Forge, received these courageous Quaker women in the most cordial manner, kept them to dinner, and for the rest of the day they were entertained by the General's wife. Through this lady's kindly intercession, all the Quakers were released.

The joy among the members of this powerful sect over the unexpected return of their brethren is extremely great. But how Congress treated them, and, according to good information, how many unworthy and previously worthless men make up this august body is shown by the fact that it completely forgot its dignity. Congress could not pass silently over this insult, yet, at the same time it could not praise enough the great justice of General Washington. And this praise is not unique; everyone is captivated by this general.

BENJAMIN RUSH TO DAVID RAMSAY [19]

November 5, 1778

General Lee's trial is the common subject of conversation in this place. The sentence of the court-martial is now before Congress. They dare not confirm it, for the proceedings of the court which are printed not only show that Lee is innocent of the charges brought against him, but that he saved our army and country on the 28th of June. They dare not reverse it, for this would impeach the veracity and candor of our commander in chief, and he possesses nearly as much influence over the resolutions of our Congress as the King of Britain does over the acts of the British Parliament. DeWit and Barnevelt were sacrificed to the excessive influence and popularity of a stadholder. They suffered death. We repine upon the cruelty of the mob of Amsterdam. We destroy *reputation,* which is dearer to a military man than life itself. CONWAY, MIFFLIN, and LEE were sacrificed to the excessive influence and popularity of *one man.* They were the first characters in the army and are all honest men. Where is the republican spirit of our country? For my part, I wish to see something

[19] Butterfield, ed., *Letters of Benjamin Rush,* I, 219–20.

like the ostracism of the Athenians introduced among us. Monarchies are illuminated by a *sun,* but republics should be illuminated only by *constellations* of great men.

BENJAMIN FRANKLIN TO GEORGE WASHINGTON [20]

March 5, 1780

Should peace arrive after another campaign or two, and afford us a little leisure, I should be happy to see your Excellency in Europe and to accompany you, if my age and strength would permit, in visiting some of its ancient and most famous kingdoms. You would, on this side of the sea, enjoy the great reputation you have acquired, pure and free from those little shades that the jealousy and envy of a man's countrymen and contemporaries are ever endeavoring to cast over living merit. Here you would know, and enjoy, what posterity will say of Washington. For a thousand leagues have nearly the same effect with a thousand years. The feeble voice of those grovelling passions cannot extend so far either in time or distance. At present I enjoy that pleasure for you; as I frequently hear the old generals of this martial country, who study the maps of America. and mark upon them all your operations, speak with sincere approbation and great applause of your conduct, and join in giving you the character of one of the greatest captains of the age.

EZEKIEL CORNELL TO WILLIAM GREENE [21]

August 1, 1780

The necessity of appointing General Washington sole dictator of America, is again talked of as the only means under God by which we can be saved from destruction.

ALEXANDER HAMILTON TO JAMES MCHENRY [22]

February, 1781

The Great man and I have come to an open rupture. Proposals of accommodation have been made on his part, but re-

---

[20] Jared Sparks, ed., *The Works of Benjamin Franklin* (Boston, 1839), VIII, 429–30.

[21] Burnett, ed., *Letters,* V, 305.

[22] Allan M. Hamilton, *The Intimate Life of Alexander Hamilton* (New York, 1910), pp. 261–62n.

jected. I pledge my honor to you that he will find me inflexible. He shall for once at least repent his ill-humor. Without a shadow of reason and on the slightest grounds—he charged me in the most affrontive manner with treating him with disrespect. I answered very decisively "Sir, I am not conscious of it, but since you have thought it necessary to tell me, so we part!" . . . We have often spoken freely our sentiments to each other. Except to a very few friends our difference will be a secret, therefore be silent.

ALEXANDER HAMILTON TO PHILIP SCHUYLER [23]

February 18, 1781

I always disliked the office of an aid-de-camp as having in it a kind of personal dependence. I refused to serve in this capacity with two major-generals at an early period of the war. Infected, however, with the enthusiasm of the times, an idea of the General's character (which experience taught me to be unfounded) overcame my scruples, and induced me to *accept his invitation* to enter into his family. It was not long before I discovered he was neither remarkable for delicacy nor good temper, which revived my former aversion to the station in which I was acting, and it has been increasing ever since. . . .

I believe you know the place I held in the General's confidence and counsels, which will make it the more extraordinary to you to learn that for three years past I have felt no friendship for him and have professed none. The truth is, our dispositions are the opposite of each other, and the pride of my temper would not suffer me to profess what I did not feel. Indeed, when advances of this kind have been made to me on his part, they were received in a manner that showed at least that I had no desire to court them, and that I desired to stand rather upon a footing of military confidence than of private attachment. . . .

The General is a very honest man. His competitors have slender abilities, and less integrity. His popularity has often been essential to the safety of America, and is still of great importance to it. These considerations have influenced my past conduct respecting him, and will influence my future. I think it is necessary he should be supported.

[23] Henry C. Lodge, ed., *The Works of Alexander Hamilton* (New York, 1880), VIII, 37–38.

JOURNAL OF BARON LUDWIG VON CLOSEN [24]

March 13, 1781

Throughout my career under General Washington, I had ample opportunity to note his *gentle* and *affable* nature; his *very simple* manners, his *very easy* accessibility; his *even* temper, his great *presence of mind,* in sum, it is evident that he is a *great man* and a *brave one.* He can never be praised sufficiently. In military matters, he does not have the brilliance of the French in *expression,* but he is *penetrating in his calculations* and a *true soldier in his bearing.* This is the opinion of the entire army, which no one can applaud more sincerely than I.

DIARY OF BARON CROMOT DUBOURG [25]

July 5, 1781

General Washington came to see M. de Rochambeau. Notified of his approach, we mounted our horses and went out to meet him. He received us with the affability which is natural to him and depicted on his countenance. He is a very fine looking man, but did not surprise me as much as I expected from the descriptions I had heard of him. His physiognomy is noble in the highest degree, and his manners are those of one perfectly accustomed to society, quite a rare thing certainly in America.

THOMAS MCKEAN TO GEORGE WASHINGTON [26]

October 31, 1781

It affords me ineffable pleasure to present to your Excellency the *Thanks* of the United States in Congress assembled, for the distinguished services you have rendered to your country, and particularly for the conquest of Lord Cornwallis and the British garrisons of York and Gloucester, and the wisdom and prudence manifested in the capitulation. . . .

[24] Evelyn M. Acomb, ed., *The Revolutionary Journal of Baron Ludwig Von Closen, 1780–1783* (Chapel Hill: The University of North Carolina Press, 1958), p. 64. The selections from this book are reprinted by permission of the publisher.

[25] *The Magazine of American History, with Notes and Queries,* IV (New York, 1880), 296.

[26] Burnett, ed., *Letters,* VI, 252–53.

Words fail me when I attempt to bestow my small tribute of thanks and praise to a character so eminent for wisdom, courage and patriotism, and one who appears to be no less the favorite of Heaven than of his country. I shall only therefore beg you to be assured, that you are held in the most grateful remembrance, and with a peculiar veneration, by all the wise and good in these United States.

That you may long possess this happiness; that you may be enabled speedily to annihilate the British power in America, which you have so effectually broken by this last capital blow; that you may be ever hailed the Deliverer of your Country, and enjoy every blessing Heaven can bestow, is . . . [my] sincere and ardent prayer.

DIARY OF FREDERICK MACKENZIE [27]

November 22, 1781

Some [British] officers came in by land from Virginia [to New York]. Mr. Washington has made it a great favor to grant any indulgence of this kind to the Officers taken at Yorktown. I think his behavior to the Officers taken there has been brutish and scandalous to the last degree, and shows that he takes every opportunity of gratifying his private resentment against the British troops. Nothing can be a stronger proof of this than his crowding above 100 British Officers, with everything belonging to them, on board one transport ship, that had been sunk during the seige, and was only raised again a few days before the Officers were sent on board her; then sending her to sea at this season of the year, with only 28 days provisions and water, to make a voyage from Chesapeake to New York, when from her being so very light, and the prevailing winds at this season, it was hardly possible she could make the passage. . . . It is not uncharitable to suppose that Mr. Washington cared very little whether any of them ever reached this place. If he had acted upon any generous principle, he would have given permission to such as chose it, to go through the country.

[27] *Diary of Frederick MacKenzie: Giving a Daily Narrative of His Military Service as an Officer of the Regiment of Royal Welch Fusiliers During the Years 1775–1781 in Massachusetts, Rhode Island and New York* (Cambridge: Harvard University Press, 1930), II, 699–700. Reprinted by permission of the publisher.

JOURNAL OF BARON LUDWIG VON CLOSEN [28]

September 20, 1782

General Washington reviewed our army and watched it march past him. He seemed to be delighted with it, and expressed his great satisfaction with it. It is impossible for those who know the General not to have the highest opinion of his *gentle, calm,* and *stately* bearing, which distinguishes him in every gathering. As for his military talents and knowledge, he gave such striking evidence of them during many of his conversations with M. de Rochambeau concerning our profession, when I was continuously present as interpreter, that I could not find strong enough words to describe them as vividly and forcefully as I should.

MARQUIS DE LAFAYETTE TO GEORGE WASHINGTON [29]

February 5, 1783

Were you but such a man as Julius Caesar, or the King of Prussia, I should almost be sorry for you at the end of the great tragedy where you are acting such a part. But, with my dear General, I rejoice at the blessings of a peace where our noble ends have been secured. Remember our Valley Forge times; and, from a recollection of past dangers and labors, we shall be still more pleased at our present comfortable situation. What a sense of pride and satisfaction I feel, when I think of the times that have determined my engaging in the American cause!

As for you, my dear General, who truly can say you have done all this, what must your virtuous and good heart feel, on the happy instant when the revolution you have made is now firmly established! I cannot but envy the happiness of my grandchildren, when they will be about celebrating and worshipping your name. To have one of their ancestors among your soldiers, to know he had the good fortune to be the friend of your heart, will be the eternal honor in which they shall glory; and to the eldest of them, as long as my posterity will last, I shall delegate the favor you have been pleased to confer upon my son George.

[28] Acomb, ed., *The Revolutionary Journal of Baron Ludwig Von Closen, 1780–1783,* p. 241.

[29] Sparks, ed., *Correspondence of the American Revolution,* III, 545–46.

JOURNAL OF ADJUTANT GENERAL MAJOR BAURMEISTER
OF THE HESSIAN FORCES [30]

October, 1783

General Washington lives near Princeton, like a private individual. If, as is generally said, he gave prestige to the American army, it is certain that his frequent presence near Princeton is lending some dignity and respect to the declining Congress. As a matter of fact this great council has never been so little respected and revered as it now is, especially in New England, where the prescribed taxes cannot be collected. This is now also the case in Pennsylvania, where Congress's flight from Philadelphia is considered an unpardonable mistake. Besides, the Pennsylvanians were the first to realize that the members of Congress were misappropriating the money gained from the sale of confiscated property.

In view of the present misgovernment, General Washington could obtain anything he might want, even the crown of North America. The people are ready to offer it to him, but so far he has shown no desire for this gift of fortune, if, indeed, it is one.

ADDRESS OF THE CITIZENS OF NEW YORK WHO HAVE
RETURNED FROM EXILE TO GENERAL WASHINGTON [31]

November 26, 1783

Sir: At a moment when the arm of tyranny is yielding up its fondest usurpations, we hope the salutations of long suffering Exiles, but now happy Freemen, will not be deemed an unworthy tribute. In this place, and at this moment of exultation and triumph, while the Ensigns of Slavery still linger in our sight, we look up to you our deliverer, with unusual transports of gratitude and joy. Permit us to welcome you to this City, long torn from us by the hard hand of oppression, but now, by your wisdom and energy, under the guidance of Providence, once more the seat of peace and freedom; we forebear to speak our gratitude or your praise. We should but echo the voice of applauding millions. But the citizens of New York are eminently indebted to your virtues and we who have now the honor to address your Excellency, have

[30] Uhlendorf, ed., *Revolution in America*, pp. 589–90.
[31] Hugh Hastings, ed., *Public Papers of George Clinton* (Albany, 1904), VIII, 300–1.

been often companions of your sufferings, and witness of your exertions. Permit us, therefore, to approach your Excellency with the dignity and sincerity of freemen, and to assure you, that we shall preserve with our last breath, our gratitude for your services, and veneration for your character; and accept of our sincere and earnest wishes that you may long enjoy the calm domestic felicity which you have so generously sacrified; that the cries of injured liberty may never more interrupt your repose, and that your happiness may be equal to your virtues.

JOURNAL OF REV. THOMAS COKE [32]

May 26, 1785

Mr. [Francis] Asbury and I set off for General Washington's. . . . the General's seat is very elegant; built upon the great river Potomac; for the improvement of the navigation of which, he is carrying on jointly with the State some amazing plans. He received us very politely, and was very open to access. He is quite the plain, country-gentleman. After dinner we desired a private interview, and opened to him the grand business on which we came, presenting to him our petition for the emancipation of the Negroes, and entreating his signature, if the eminence of his station did not render it inexpedient for him to sign any petition. He informed us that he was of our sentiments, and had signified his thoughts on the subject to most of the great men of the State; that he did not see it proper to sign the petition, but if the Assembly took it into consideration, would signify his sentiments to the Assembly by a letter.

NOTES OF WILLIAM PIERCE [33]

May, 1787

General Washington is well known as the commander in chief of the late American army. Having conducted these states to independence and peace, he now appears to assist in framing a government to make the people happy. Like Gustavus Vasa, he may be said to be the deliverer of this country; like Peter the Great he appears as the politician and the statesman; and like Cincinnatus he returned to his farm perfectly contented with being only

---

[32] *The Magazine of American History*, IV, 158.
[33] "Notes of William Pierce on the Federal Convention of 1787," *The American Historical Review*, III (1897–98), 331.

a plain citizen after enjoying the highest honor of the confederacy —and now only seeks for the approbation of his countrymen by being virtuous and useful. The General was conducted to the Chair as President of the [Constitutional] Convention by the unanimous voice of its members. He is in the 52nd year of his age.

"PHILADELPHIENSIS" [34]

January 14–21, 1788

It was a common saying among many sensible men in Great Britain and Ireland, in the time of the war, that they doubted whether the great men of America, who had taken an active part in favor of independence, were influenced by pure patriotism; that it was not the love of their country they had so much at heart, as their own private interest; that a thirst after dominion and power, and not to protect the oppressed from the oppressor, was the great operative principle that induced these men to oppose Britain so strenuously. This seemingly illiberal sentiment was, however, generally denied by the well-hearted and unsuspecting friends of American liberty in Europe, who could not suppose that men would engage in so noble a cause thro' such base motives. But alas! The truth of the sentiment is now indisputably confirmed; facts are stubborn things, and these set the matter beyond controversy. The new Constitution and the conduct of its despotic advocates, show that these men's doubts were really well founded. Unparalleled duplicity! That men should oppose tyranny under a pretence of patriotism, that they might themselves become the tyrants. How does such villainy disgrace human nature! Ah, my fellow citizens, you have been strangely deceived indeed; when the wealthy of your own country assisted you to expel the foreign tyrant, only with a view to substitute themselves in his stead.

"YEOMANRY OF MASSACHUSETTS" [35]

January 25, 1788

Another thing they tell us, that the Constitution must be good from the characters which composed the Convention that

[34] "Philadelphiensis," in the Boston *American Herald,* January 14, 21, 1788, from a Philadelphia newspaper, quoted in Morton Borden, ed., *The Antifederalist Papers* (East Lansing, 1965), p. 108.

[35] "Yeomanry of Massachusetts," in *The Massachusetts Gazette,* January 25, 1788, quoted in Borden, ed., *The Antifederalists Papers,* pp. 111–12.

framed it. It is graced with the names of a Washington and a Franklin. Illustrious names, we know—worthy characters in civil society. Yet we cannot suppose them to be infallible guides; neither yet a man must necessarily incur guilt to himself merely by dissenting from them in opinion.

We cannot think the noble general has the same ideas with ourselves, with regard to the rules of right and wrong. We cannot think he acts a very consistent part, or did through the whole of the contest with Great Britain. Notwithstanding he wielded the sword, in defense of American liberty, yet at the same time was, and is to this day, living upon the labors of several hundreds of miserable Africans, as free born as himself; and some of them very likely, descended from parents who, in point of property and dignity in their own country, might cope with any man in America. We do not conceive we are to be overborne by the weight of any names, however revered.

JOURNAL OF WILLIAM MACLAY [36]

June 11, 1789

I have ever been very attentive to discover, if possible, General Washington's private opinions on the pompous part of government. His address of "fellow citizens" to the two Houses of Congress seems quite republican. Mrs. Morris, however, gave us something on this subject. General Washington, on a visit to her, *had declared himself in the most pointed manner for generous salaries; and added that, without large salaries, proper persons could never be got to fill the offices of government with propriety.* He might deliver something of this kind with propriety enough without using the word "large." However, if he lives with the pompous people of New York, he must be something more than human if their high-toned manners have not some effect on him.

June 18, 1789

I have ever been as attentive as I possibly could be to discover the real disposition of President Washington. He has been very cautious hitherto, or rather inactive, or shall I say like a pupil in the hands of his governor or a child in the arms of his nurse? . . . I entertain no doubt but that many people are aiming with

[36] Edgar S. Maclay, ed., *Journal of William Maclay* (New York, 1890), pp. 74, 82, 122–23, 131, 176–77, 206, 248–49, 351.

all their force to establish a splendid court with all the pomp of majesty. Alas! poor Washington, if you are taken in this snare! How will the gold become dim! How will the fine gold be changed! How will your glory fade!

August 16, 1789

A conference has been held with the President, in which Mr. Izard declares that the President owned he had consulted the members of the House of Representatives as to his nominations, but likewise said he had not acted so with the Senators, as they could have an opportunity of giving their advice and consent afterward. This small anecdote serves to divulge his [Washington's] conduct, or rather to fix my opinion of his conduct, for some time past, to wit, a courtship of and attention to the House of Representatives, that by their weight he may depress the Senate and exalt his perogatives [sic] on the ruins. Mr. Izard was clearly of the opinion that all the late measures flowed from the President. Mr. Madison, in his opinion, was deep in this business. The President showed great want of temper (as Izard said) when one of his nominations was rejected. The President may, however, be considered as in a great measure passive in the business. The creatures that surround him would place a crown on his head, that they may have the handling of its jewels.

August 22, 1789

I can not now be mistaken. The President wishes to tread on the necks of the Senate.

January 14, 1790

It is evident from the President's speech that he wishes everything to fall into the British mode of business. "I have directed the proper officers to lay before you," etc. Compliments for him and business for them. He is but a man, but really a good one, and we can have nothing to fear from him, but much from the precedents he may establish.

Dined this day with the President. It was a great dinner—all in the taste of high life. I considered it as a part of my duty as a Senator to submit to it, and am glad it is over. The President is a cold, formal man; but I must declare that he treated me with great attention. I was the first person with whom he drank a glass of wine. I was often spoken to by him. Yet he knows how rigid a republican I am. I can not think that he considers it worth while to soften me. It is not worth his while. I am not an object if he should gain me, and I trust he can not do it by any improper means.

March 4, 1790

Dined with the President of the United States. It was a dinner of dignity. All the Senators were present, and the Vice-President. I looked often around the company to find the happiest faces. Wisdom, forgive me if I wrong thee, but I thought folly and happiness most nearly allied. The President seemed to bear in his countenance a settled aspect of melancholy. No cheering ray of convivial sunshine broke through the cloudy gloom of settled seriousness. At every interval of eating or drinking he played on the table with a fork or knife, like a drumstick. Next to him, on his right, sat Bonny Johnny Adams, ever and anon mantling his visage with the most unmeaning simper that ever dimpled the face of folly.

April 26, 1790

Dr. Elmer asked me to walk with him. I saw cards handed about the Senate, but this happens so often that I took no notice of it. When we were in the street the doctor asked me if I had not a card to dine with the President. I told him, with all the indifference I could put on, no, and immediately took up some other subject, which I entered upon with eagerness, as if I had hardly noticed his question. This is the second time the Doctor has asked me the same question, so that the President's neglect of me can be no secret. How unworthy of a great character is such littleness! He [Washington] is not aware, however, that he is paying me a compliment that none of his guests can claim. He places me above the influence of a dinner, even in his own opinion. Perhaps he means it as a punishment for my opposition to court measures. Either way, I care not a fig for it. I certainly feel a pride arising from a consciousness that the greatest man in the world has not credit enough with me to influence my conduct in the least.

December 14, 1790

This was levee day, and I accordingly dressed and did the needful. It is an idle thing, but what is the life of men but folly?

And this is perhaps as innocent as any of them, so far as respects the persons acting. The practice, however, considered as a feature of royalty, is certainly anti-republican. This certainly escapes nobody. The royalists glory in it as a point gained. Republicans are borne down by fashion and a fear of being charged with a want of respect to General Washington. If there is treason in the wish I retract it, but would to God this same General Washington were in heaven! We would not then have him brought forward as the constant cover to every unconstitutional and irrepublican act.

JOHN ADAMS TO BENJAMIN RUSH [37]

April 4, 1790

The history of our Revolution will be one continued Lie from one end to the other. The essence of the whole will be *that Dr. Franklin's electrical rod smote the earth and out sprung General Washington. That Franklin electrified him with his rod—and thence forward these two conducted all the policy, negotiations legislatures, and war.* These underscored lines contain the whole fable, plot and catastrophe. If this letter should be preserved, and read a hundred years hence, the reader will say, "the envy of this John Adams could not bear to think of the Truth. He ventured to scribble to Rush, as envious as himself, blasphemy that he dared not speak when he lived. But barkers at the sun and moon are always silly curs."

REPUBLICAN ESSAYIST [38]

1795

The President, not content with annihilating the people [in the Whiskey rebellion], wishes also to annihilate the obligations of the treaty [of 1778 with France]—the price of our liberties. Faithless, unprincipled, and aristocratical moderatist, who would offer up the liberties of thy fellow-citizens on the altar of Administration, and the sacred obligations of our country, though perhaps not thine, on the altar of treachery and dishonor!

How long is this to be borne with? How long are we to submit to the exertions of a set of people among us, who wish to pros-

[37] *Old Family Letters: Copied from the Originals for Alexander Biddle* (Philadelphia, 1892), pp. 55–56.
[38] Quoted in William Cobbett, *Porcupine's Works* (London, 1801), I, 399.

trate us at the feet of Great Britain, and barter away everything freemen hold dear? Is there not one propitious gale to kindle the expiring embers of liberty again to consume its conspirators? Disguised moderatists, beware! Freemen are slow to anger; but, when roused, moderation and forbearance may forsake them.

DIARY OF DR. NATHANIEL AMES [39]

August 14, 1795

The President Washington ratified the Treaty with Britain, and Hammond, the British Minister here, immediately sailed for England. Washington now defies the whole Sovereign [people] that made him what he is—and can unmake him again. Better his hand had been cut off when his glory was at its height, before he blasted all his laurels.

LETTERS TO THE PHILADELPHIA AURORA [40]

"Belisarius"

September 15, 1795

Believe me, Sir, your fellow citizens are not mere moulds of wax, calculated to receive any impression which the *dicta* of a magistrate may attempt to make upon them; neither are they too timid to resist, or too shortsighted to detect the imposition; and however you may attempt to clothe your responses to their applications in mystery and empiricism, they will not regard you as a priest, a prophet, or a demigod. An affectation of parable may please your flatterers, but it is only disgusting to men of sense, and can never deceive your countrymen. Stript of the mantle of infallibility, and possessing nought of the *jus divinum,* you appear before them a frail mortal, whose passions and weaknesses are like those of other men.

"A Communication"

September 17, 1795

The French have not been wholly inattentive to the progress of our government to a state of aristocratic *maturity.* They have

---

[39] Charles Warren, *Jacobin and Junto, or Early American Politics as Viewed in the Diary of Dr. Nathaniel Ames, 1785–1822* (Cambridge: Harvard University Press, 1931), p. 63. Reprinted by permission of the publisher.

[40] Philadelphia *Aurora and General Advertiser.*

seen the causes: they have rightly judged the President's undue popularity to be one, and have considered his policy in refusing the salary allowed him to have been one of the *little* means used to buoy up that popularity.

His conduct in this respect, however, has more in it than at first meets the eye. He will not accept the salary, but only charge the treasury with the amount of his expenses; then those expenses are made to swallow up the whole 25,000 dollars. So that, disinterestedness glares in the front, the popularity of his character gets the fillip intended, and the treasury is not a farthing the richer for the sacrifice. Even these trifles are well worth guarding against in a constitution, for aristocracy is so pliable and ferretting that it will creep in at the smallest chink.

"Pittachus"

September 18, 1795

It is said the President values himself in his *firmness,* and that as he began the treaty, this quality would prompt him to go through with it. But it will be remembered that what may be called firmness in a good cause is obstinacy in a bad one, and that a perseverance in virtue may command respect, but a pertinacity in wrong must ensure disgust and detestation.

"Portius"

September 30, 1795

At the dissolution of the American army, you had declared that you would not accept of any office under the government. This no doubt was your determination—America had no office to give worthy of your acceptance. A Governor of a State was beneath the dignity of a Commander in Chief, and a President of Congress was still more contemptible. You retired from public life perhaps because public life could not gratify your ambition; for this country did not yet offer the opportunity of imitating monarchical splendor, or of exercising regal power. It was, however, to this resignation that you owed so great an increase of your popularity. It was supposed that he who could forego an opportunity of placing himself on the throne must be more than man. It was imagined that the late army would and could have declared you a king. . . . You rejected the temptation, perhaps from the danger of the attempt, and to secure the fame which your forebearance gave, was one probable reason for your refusal to receive any compensation for your military services, other than defraying the expenses of your camp family. Is virtue then so scarce? Is human nature so debased that a man is exalted into a demigod because he was not an open traitor? An endeavor to enslave us by the army might have produced civil war, but must have ended in the deserved punishment of the Commander who would attempt it. If avoiding a hazardous enterprise entitles a man to any character for virtue, it is for the virtue of prudence. You are, perhaps, the only person who ever acquired fame by shrinking from an attempt which must have been unsuccessful.

"Casca"

October 23, 1795

The House of Representatives must either impeach [Washington] or renounce their sacred duties, apostatize from their pure principles, and reject the supplications, and despise the mandates of their injured constituents. I will examine what charges will probably compose this impeachment, as a matter of curious speculation.

1st. Instead of exercising the qualified veto entrusted to him for the preservation of liberty, so as to restrain aristocratical innovations, and to prevent dangerous institutions, he expressly sanctioned the Funding System, the Assumption, the Bank, and all the rest of the long train of legislative evils, of which we complain so justly.

2nd. He has patronized the enemies of the people with an ardor which appears to demonstrate congeniality of sentiment and unity of design.

3rd. He has formed a close and suspicious union with the despot whose Generals he vanquished in the field, and whose machinations he ought ever to have opposed in the Cabinet.

4th. He has manifested an hostility to the brave Republic which has contended for the Rights of Man against all the tyrants of the earth. . . .

5th. He proscribed the Democratic Societies, those centinels of liberty, nearly at the same moment George the Third repeated the philippic taught him with much difficulty by Mr. Pitt, against the "self-created societies" in England.

6th. He exercised legislative power through the medium of a proclamation [of neutrality], justifiable only under absurd pretexts, and most criminal in its real motives.

7th. He forced the philosophic patriot [Jefferson] who first occupied the Department of State to abandon the service of his country and to seek an humble retirement.

8th. He has administered the executive department upon principles incompatible with the spirit of republican constitution, and on precedents derived from the corrupt government of England, a government contrived to produce the greatest possible quantity of wealth, splendor and power for the *governors,* and to excite the superlative degree of credulity and ignorance in the *governed.*

9th. He indirectly superseded the various resolutions brought forward in Congress to obtain compensation for British injustice by unconstitutionally appointing our Chief Justice [Jay] minion and parasite extraordinary and plenipotentiary to the Court of St. James.

10th. He secured the adoption of the Treaty procured by the complaisance of this most honorable ambassador, by tenderly concealing its hideous features from the public eye.

11th. He saw without one single emotion of "sensibility," without one single sensation of patriotism, his country before him in the humblest attitude of entreaty, earnestly supplicating him not to surrender her property, her hopes, and her liberty, to the tyrant from whose chains she had just escaped.

12th. He has destroyed the Constitution by the ratification of a Treaty which could only have been signed upon the principle that all those powers were vested in the President and Senate which were given to Congress.

13th. He has submitted to the insults and to the injuries which his country has received, with a passiveness which would have dishonored the administration of an Oriental Queen.

14th. He shrunk from a contest in which his country would have obtained glory, to wage a despicable war with the savages of the desert, that might employ the attention and expand the debt of his country.

15th. He ostentatiously exerted that military force against a few deluded citizens [the Whiskey Rebellion], whom reason would soon have brought back to their duty, which he ought to have directed against the haughty enemy who had invaded our territory, and plundered our merchants in every part of the globe.

16th. He maintained a standing army under the absurd pretext of preventing a return of that spirit of insurrection which has been extinguished forever by the genius of Republican virtue.

17th. The firmness which he once possessed has degenerated into haughtiness to his fellow citizens and their allies, and the caution which once saved his country is degenerated into cowardice to its inveterate enemies.

When all these circumstances are combined, an awful conclusion bursts upon the understanding. . . . An impeachment must appear requisite.

A Calm Observer

October 23, 1795

Will not the world be led to conclude that the mask of hypocrisy has been alike worn by a CAESAR, a CROMWELL, and a WASHINGTON?

ISAAC WELD [41]

February 22, 1796

Not one town of any importance was there in the whole union, where some meeting did not take place in honor of this day [Washington's birthday]; yet singular as it may appear, there are people in the country, Americans too, foremost in boasting to other nations of that Constitution, which has been raised for them by his valor and wisdom, who are either so insensible to his merit, or so totally devoid of every generous sentiment, that they can refuse to join in commendations of those talents to which they are so much indebted; indeed to such a length has this perverse spirit been carried, that I have myself seen numbers of men, in all other points men of respectability, that have peremptorily refused even to pay him the small compliment of drinking to his health after dinner; it is true indeed, that they qualify their conduct partly by asserting, that it is only as President of the United States, and not as General Washington, that they have a dislike to him; but this is only a mean subterfuge, which they are forced to have recourse to, lest their conduct should appear

[41] Isaac Weld, *Travels Through the States of North America, and the Provinces of Upper and Lower Canada during the Years 1795, 1796, and 1797* (London, 1800), I, 107–9.

too strongly marked with ingratitude. During the war there were many, and not loyalists either, who were doing all in their power to remove him from that command whereby he so eminently dis-tinguished himself. It is the spirit of dissatisfaction which forms a leading trait in the character of the Americans as a people, which produces this malevolence at present, just at it did formerly; and if their public affairs were regulated by a person sent from heaven, I firmly believe his acts, instead of meeting with universal appro-bation, would by many be considered as deceitful and flagitious.

OLIVER WOLCOTT SR. TO OLIVER WOLCOTT [42]

October 3, 1796

The President's declining to be again elected constitutes a most important epoch in our national affairs. The country meet the event with reluctance, but they do not feel that they can make any claim for the further services of a man who has conducted to establish a national government, has so long presided over our councils and directed the public administration, and has, in the most advantageous manner, settled all national differences, and who can leave the administration when nothing but our folly and internal discord can render the country otherwise than happy. His secession from the administration will probably, within no dis-tant period, ascertain whether our present system and union can be preserved. It may exist a few years, but the violent symptoms which have attacked it so early, evince to my mind that it will be but of short duration. We have not the least evidence that this is the age of reason. The retirement of the President will induce among many, very serious reflections, and his advice to his coun-try, which is the best which could possibly be given, will be much read and will make a pretty strong temporary impression; but like all other advice, however good, will not be lasting. Pride and ambition, supported by ignorance and vice, will not be confined within the limits he has prescribed.

The extreme scurrility and abuse with which the President has been treated, gives an additional proof of human baseness. Con-stant reiterations of this kind, suffered to pass with impunity, would lead to debase the character of an angel. As reluctant as I feel at the retirement of the President, I believe, upon reflection, it is

---

[42] George Gibbs, *Memoirs of the Administrations of Washington and John Adams* (New York, 1846), I, 385–86.

probable he has chosen the proper time, both for himself and the country. Matters will be brought to a test. If Jefferson shall supply his place, which I trust will not be the case, however plausible his conduct will be, he never will have the northern confidence. Literary abilities and practical knowledge are not frequently conjoined, and he never will be thought to act but under the veil of hypocrisy. The politics which he has adopted and which he will always insidiously support, are inconsistent with the honor and safety of our country, and his mind is too limited not to act under a partial bias.

HENRY KNOX TO GEORGE WASHINGTON [43]

January 15, 1797

For your own sake, I rejoice at the near approach of your retirement. In it, I pray God that you may enjoy all the felicity of which the human condition is susceptible. The consciousness of having acted well, would, under any circumstances, have elevated your soul above the peltings of storms raised by malice and envy. But in addition to this consciousness, the consecration of your retirement by the unlimited gratitude of your country, must present, in the decline of your life, the most perfect reward.

JOHN MARSHALL TO CONGRESS [44]

December 19, 1799

Mr. Speaker: The melancholy event which was yesterday announced with doubt, has been rendered too certain. Our WASHINGTON is no more! The Hero, the Sage, and the Patriot of America—the man on whom in times of danger every eye was turned and all hopes were placed—lives now only in his own great actions, and in the hearts of an affectionate and afflicted people. If, sir, it has even not been usual openly to testify respect for the memory of those whom Heaven had selected as its instrument for dispensing good to men, yet such has been the uncommon worth, and such the extraordinary incidents, which have marked the life of him whose loss we all deplore, that the American Nation, impelled by the same feelings, would call with one voice

[43] Sparks, ed., *Correspondence of the American Revolution*, IV, 494.

[44] Albert Beveridge, *The Life of John Marshall* (Boston: Houghton Mifflin Company, 1916), II, 440–42. Reprinted by permission of the publisher.

for a public manifestation of that sorrow which is so deep and so universal. More than any other individual, and as much as to one individual was possible, has he contributed to found this our wide-spread empire, and to give to the Western World its independence and its freedom. Having effected the great object for which he was placed at the head of our armies, we have seen him converting the sword into the plough-share, and voluntarily sinking the soldier in the citizen.

When the debility of our federal system had become manifest, and the bonds which connected the parts of this vast continent were dissolving, we have seen him the Chief of those patriots who formed for us a Constitution, which, by preserving the Union, will, I trust, substantiate and perpetuate those blessings our Revolution had promised to bestow. In obedience to the general voice of his country, calling on him to preside over a great people, we have seen him once more quit the retirement he loved, and in a season more stormy and tempestuous than war itself, with calm and wise determination, pursue the true interests of the Nation, and contribute, more than any other could contribute, to the establishment of that system of policy which will, I trust, yet preserve our peace, our honor and our independence. Having been twice unanimously chosen the Chief Magistrate of a free people, we see him, at a time when his re-election with the universal suffrage could not have been doubted, affording to the world a rare instance of moderation, by withdrawing from his high station to the peaceful walks of private life. However the public confidence may change, and the public affections fluctuate with respect to others, yet with respect to him they have in war and in peace, in public and in private life, been as steady as his own firm mind, and as constant as his own exalted virtues. . . .

EDITORIAL "COLUMBIA MOURNS" [45]

December 21, 1799

It is with the deepest grief that we announce to the public the death of our *most distinguished* fellow-citizen *Lieut. General George Washington*. He died at Mount Vernon on Saturday evening, the 13th inst. of an inflammatory infection of the throat, which put a period to his existence in 23 hours.

The grief which we suffer on this truly mournful occasion, would

[45] *New York Gazette and General Advertiser*, December 21, 1799.

be in some degree, alleviated, if we possessed abilities to do justice to the merits of this *illustrious benefactor of mankind;* but conscious of our inferiority, we shrink from the sublimity of the subject. To the impartial and eloquent historian, therefore, we consign the high and grateful office of exhibiting the life of *George Washington* to the present age, and to generations yet unborn, as a perfect model of all that is *virtuous, noble, great,* and *dignified* in man. Our feelings, however, will not permit us to forbear observing, that the very disinterested and important services rendered by *George Washington* to these United States, both in the Field and in the Cabinet, have erected in the hearts of his countrymen monuments of sincere and unbounded gratitude, which the mouldering hand of Time cannot deface; and that in every quarter of the Globe, where a free Government is ranked amongst the choice blessings of Providence, and *virtue, morality, religion,* and *patriotism* are respected, THE NAME of WASHINGTON will be held in *veneration.*

ALEXANDER HAMILTON TO TOBIAS LEAR [46]

January 2, 1800

Perhaps no man in this community has equal cause with myself to deplore the loss [of Washington]. I have been much indebted to the kindness of the General, and he was an *Aegis very essential to me.* But regrets are unavailing. For great misfortunes it is the business of reason to seek consolation. The friends of General Washington have very noble ones. If virtue can secure happiness in another world, he is happy. In this the seal is now put upon *his* glory. It is no longer in jeopardy from the fickleness of fortune.

P. S. In whose hands are his papers gone? Our very confidential situation will not permit this to be a point of indifference to me.

GOUVERNEUR MORRIS TO JOHN MARSHALL[47]

June 26, 1807

In approving highly your character of Washington, permit me to add that few men of such steady, persevering industry ever

[46] Lodge, *Hamilton,* VIII, 538.
[47] Anne Cary Morris, ed., *The Diary and Letters of Gouverneur Morris* (New York, 1888), II, 492.

existed, and perhaps no one who so completely commanded himself. Thousands have learned to restrain their passions, though few among them had to contend with passions so violent. But the self-command to which I allude was of higher grade. He could, at the dictate of reason, control his will and command himself to act. Others may have acquired a portion of the same authority; but who could, like Washington, at any moment command the energies of his mind to a cheerful exertion?

JOHN ADAMS TO BENJAMIN RUSH [48]

November 11, 1807

Our Hero was much indebted to his talents for "his immense elevation above his fellows." Talents! You will say, what talents? I answer:

1. A handsome face. That this is a talent I can prove by the authority of a thousand instances in all ages. . . .

2. A tall stature, like the Hebrew sovereign chosen because he was taller by a head than the other Jews.

3. An elegant form.

4. Graceful attitudes and movements.

5. A large imposing fortune consisting of a great landed estate left him by his father and brother, besides a large jointure with his lady, and the guardianship of the heirs of the great Custis estate, and in addition to all this, immense tracts of land of his own acquisition. There is nothing, except bloody battles and splendid victories to which mankind bow down with more reverence than to great fortune. . . .

6. Washington was a Virginian. This is equivalent to five talents. Virginia geese are all swans. . . . Not a lad upon the High Lands [of Scotland] is more clannish than every Virginian I have ever known. They trumpet one another with the most pompous and mendacious panegyrics. The Philadelphians and New Yorkers, who are local and partial enough to themselves, are meek and modest in comparison with Virginian Old Dominionism. Washington of course was extolled without bounds.

7. Washington was preceded by favorable anecdotes. The English had used him ill in the expedition of Braddock. They had not done justice to his bravery and good council. They had ex-

[48] *Old Family Letters*, pp. 168–70.

aggerated and misrepresented his defeat and capitulation; which
interested the pride as well as compassion of Americans in his
favor. . . . Mr. Lynch of South Carolina told me before we met
in Congress in 1774 that "Colonel Washington had made the
most eloquent speech that ever had been spoken upon the controversy with England, viz., That if the English should attack the
people of Boston, he would raise a thousand men at his own expense and march at their head to New England to their aid."
Several other favorable stories preceded his appearance in Congress and in the Army.

8. He possessed the gift of silence. This I esteem as one of the
most precious talents.

9. He had great self-command. It cost him a great exertion sometimes, and a constant constraint, but to preserve so much equanimity as he did required a great capacity.

10. Whenever he lost his temper as he did sometimes, either
love or fear in those about him induced them to conceal his
weakness from the world.

Here you see I have made out ten talents without saying a word
about reading, thinking or writing. . . .

BENJAMIN RUSH TO JOHN ADAMS [49]

July 8, 1812

Among the national sins of our country that have provoked
the wrath of Heaven to afflict us with a war, I ought to have
mentioned in my last letter the idolatrous worship paid to the
name of General Washington, by all classes and nearly all parties
of our citizens, manifested in the impious application of names and
epithets to him which are ascribed in Scripture only to God
and to Jesus Christ. The following is part of them: "our Saviour,"
"our Redeemer," "our cloud by day and our pillar of fire by
night," "our star in the east," "To us a Son is born," and "our
guide on earth, our advocate in heaven." With the sin of these
epithets is connected two other sins: 1st, Ingratitude to all other
Revolutionary servants of the public in the cabinet or the field,
Alexr. Hamilton only excepted; and 2ly, a total belief in the divine
talents and virtues ascribed to him by most of his companions in
arms and contemporaries in the Revolution, more especially by
the citizens of Boston, New York, and Philadelphia who sub-

[49] Butterfield, ed., *Letters of Benjamin Rush,* II, 1146–47.

mitted to the British army during the American war. What an ocean of political turpitude has been wiped away by the ten letters that compose his name!

THOMAS JEFFERSON TO DR. WALTER JONES [50]

January 2, 1814

I think I knew General Washington intimately and thoroughly; and were I called on to delineate his character, it should be in terms like these.

His mind was great and powerful, without being of the very first order; his penetration strong, though not so acute as that of a Newton, Bacon, or Locke; and as far as he saw, no judgment was ever sounder. It was slow in operation, being little aided by invention or imagination, but sure in conclusion. Hence the common remark of his officers, of the advantage he derived from councils of war, where hearing all suggestions, he selected whatever was best; and certainly no General ever planned his battles more judiciously. But if deranged during the course of the action, if any member of his plan was dislocated by sudden circumstances, he was slow in readjustment. The consequence was, that he often failed in the field, and rarely against an enemy in station, as at Boston and York. He was incapable of fear, meeting personal dangers with the calmest unconcern. Perhaps the strongest feature in his character was prudence, never acting until every circumstance, every consideration, was maturely weighed; refraining if he saw a doubt, but, when once decided, going through with his purpose, whatever obstacles opposed. His integrity was most pure, his justice the most inflexible I have ever known, no motives of interest or consanguinity, of friendship or hatred, being able to bias his decision. He was, indeed, in every sense of the words, a wise, a good, and a great man. His temper was naturally high toned; but reflection and resolution had obtained a firm and habitual ascendency over it. If ever, however, it broke its bonds, he was most tremendous in his wrath. In his expenses he was honorable, but exact; liberal in contributions to whatever promised utility; but frowning and unyielding on all visionary projects, and all unworthy calls on his charity. His heart was not warm in its affections; but he exactly calculated every man's value, and gave

[50] Paul L. Ford, ed., *The Works of Thomas Jefferson* (New York, 1905), XI, 374–79.

him a solid esteem proportioned to it. His person, you know, was fine, his stature exactly what one would wish, his deportment easy, erect and noble; the best horseman of his age, and the most graceful figure that could be seen on horseback. Although in the circle of his friends, where he might be unreserved with safety, he took a free share in conversation, his colloquial talents were not above mediocrity, possessing neither copiousness of ideas, nor fluency of words. In public, when called on for a sudden opinion, he was unready, short and embarrassed. Yet he wrote readily, rather diffusely, in an easy and correct style. This he had acquired by conversation with the world, for his education was merely reading, writing and common arithmetic, to which he added surveying at a later day. His time was employed in action chiefly, reading little, and that only in agriculture and English history. His correspondence became necessarily extensive, and, with journalizing his agricultural proceedings, occupied most of his leisure hours within doors. On the whole, his character was, in its mass, perfect, in nothing bad, in few points indifferent; and it may truly be said, that never did nature and fortune combine more perfectly to make a man great, and to place him in the same constellation with whatever worthies have merited from man an everlasting remembrance. For his was the singular destiny and merit of leading the armies of his country successfully through an arduous war, for the establishment of its independence; of conducting its councils through the birth of a government, new in its forms and principles, until it had settled down into a quiet and orderly train; and of scrupulously obeying the laws through the whole of his career, civil and military, of which the history of the world furnishes no other example. . . .

I am satisfied the great body of republicans think of him as I do. We were, indeed, dissatisfied with him on his ratification of the British treaty. But this was short lived. We knew his honesty, the wiles with which he was encompassed, and that age had already began to relax the firmness of his purposes; and I am convinced he is more deeply seated in the love and gratitude of the republicans, than in the Pharisaical homage of the federal monarchists. For he was no monarchist from preference of his judgment. The soundness of that gave him correct views of the rights of man, and his severe justice devoted him to them. He has often declared to me that he considered our new constitution as an experiment on the practicability of republican government, and with what dose of liberty man could be trusted for his own good; that he was determined the experiment should have a fair trial, and would lose the last drop of his blood in support of it. And these declarations he repeated to me the oftener and more pointedly, because he knew my suspicions of Colonel Hamilton's views, and probably had heard from him the same declarations which I had, to wit, "that the British constitution, with its unequal representation, corruption and other existing abuses, was the most perfect government which had ever been established on earth, and that a reformation of those abuses would make it an impracticable government." I do believe that General Washington had not a firm confidence in the durability of our government. He was naturally distrustful of men, and inclined to gloomy apprehensions; and I was ever persuaded that a belief that we must at length end in something like a British constitution, had some weight in his adoption of the ceremonies of levees, birth-days, pompous meetings with Congress, and other forms of the same character, calculated to prepare us gradually for a change which he believed possible, and to let it come on with as little shock as might be to the public mind.

These are my opinions of General Washington, which I would vouch at the judgment seat of God, having been formed on an acquaintance of thirty years. I served with him in the Virginia legislature from 1769 to the Revolutionary war, and again, a short time in Congress, until he left us to take command of the army. During the war and after it we corresponded occasionally, and in the four years of my continuance in the office of Secretary of State, our intercourse was daily, confidential and cordial. After I retired from that office, great and malignant pains were taken by our federal monarchists, and not entirely without effect, to make him view me as a theorist, holding French principles of government, which would lead infallibly to licentiousness and anarchy. And to this he listened the more easily, from my known disapprobation of the British treaty. I never saw him afterwards, or these malignant insinuations should have been dissipated before his just judgment, as mists before the sun. I felt on his death, with my countrymen, that "verily a great man hath fallen this day in Israel."

WASHINGTON IN HISTORY

The ten selections which follow are arranged chronologically, and have been chosen to give the reader an idea of how Washington has been evaluated by scholars of different eras. Mason Weems, the first author, was hardly a scholar, but his work is included for its paramount role in the legend-building process. John Marshall, Francois Guizot, and Henry Tuckerman all offer appreciations of Washington's character. The appraisals by R. Ernest Dupuy and Trevor N. Dupuy, and James T. Flexner, should be compared for their analyses of Washington's military leadership. A brief excerpt from a "debunking" volume by William E. Woodward is included as a sample of that genre. Both J. A. Carroll and Thomas A. Bailey weigh Washington's performance as President. The longest selection is from the multivolume study by Douglas S. Freeman, by far the most comprehensive and distinguished modern biography of Washington.

MASON L. WEEMS [1]

"Pa (said George very seriously) do I ever tell lies?"

"No, George, I *thank God* you do not, my son; and I rejoice in the hope you never will. At least, you shall never, from me, have cause to be guilty of so shameful a thing. Many parents, indeed, even compel their children to this vile practice, by barbarously beating them for every little fault; hence, on the next offense, the little terrified creature slips out a *lie!* Just to escape the rod. But as to yourself, George, you know I have *always* told you, and now tell you again, that, whenever by accident you do any thing wrong, which must often be the case, as you are but a poor little boy yet, without *experience* or *knowledge,* never tell a falsehood to conceal it; but come *bravely* up, my son, like a *little man,* and tell

[1] Mason L. Weems, *The Life of George Washington; with Curious Anecdotes, Equally Honorable to Himself and Exemplary to His Young Countrymen,* 10th ed. (Philadelphia, 1810), pp. 13–18.

me of it; and instead of beating you, George, I will but the more honor and love you for it, my dear."

THIS, you'll say, was sowing good seed! Yes, it was: and the crop, thank God, was, as I believe it ever will be, where a man acts the true parent, that is, the *Guardian Angel,* by his child.

The following anecdote is a *case in point.* It is too valuable to be lost, and too true to be doubted; for it was communicated to me by the same excellent lady to whom I am indebted for the last.

"When George," said she, "was about six years old, he was made the wealthy master of a *hatchet!* of which, like most little boys, he was immoderately fond, and was constantly going about chopping every thing that came in his way. One day, in the garden, where he often amused himself hacking his mother's peasticks, he unluckily tried the edge of his hatchet on the body of a beautiful young English cherry-tree, which he barked so terribly, that I don't believe the tree ever got the better of it. The next morning the old gentleman finding out what had befallen his tree, which, by the by, was a great favorite, came into the house, and with much warmth asked for the mischievous author, declaring at the same time, that he would not have taken five guineas for his tree. Nobody could tell him any thing about it. Presently George and his hatchet made their appearance. 'George,' said his father, 'do you know who killed that beautiful little cherry-tree yonder in the garden?' This was a *tough question;* and George staggered under it for a moment; but quickly recovered himself: and looking at his father, with the sweet face of youth brightened with the inexpressible charm of all-conquering truth, he bravely cried out, 'I can't tell a lie, Pa; you know I can't tell a lie. I did cut it with my hatchet.' 'Run to my arms, you dearest boy,' cried his father in transports, 'run to my arms; glad am I, George, that you killed my tree; for you have paid me for it a thousand fold. Such an act of heroism in my son is more worth than a thousand trees, though blossomed with silver, and their fruits of purest gold.'"

It was in this way, by interesting at once both his *heart* and *head,* that Mr. Washington conducted George with great ease and pleasure along the happy paths of virtue. But well knowing that his beloved charge, soon to be a man, would be left exposed to numberless temptations, both from himself and from others, his heart throbbed with the tenderest anxiety to make him acquainted with that GREAT BEING, whom to know and love, is to possess the surest defence against vice, and the best of all motives to virtue and happiness. To startle George into a lively sense of his Maker, he fell upon the following very curious but impressive expedient:

ONE day he went into the garden, and prepared a little bed of finely pulverized earth, on which he wrote George's name at full, in large letters—then strewing in plenty of cabbage seed, he covered them up, and smoothed all over nicely with the roller. This bed he purposely prepared close alongside of a gooseberry walk, which happening at this time to be well hung with ripe fruit, he knew would be honored with George's visits pretty regularly every day. Not many mornings had passed away before in came George, with eyes wild rolling, and his little cheeks ready to burst with *great news.*

"O Pa! come here! come here!"

"What's the matter, my son, what's the matter?"

"O COME here, I tell you, Pa, come here! and I'll show you such a sight as you never saw in all your life time."

THE old gentleman suspecting what George would be at, gave him his hand, which he seized with great eagerness, and tugging him along through the garden, led him point blank to the bed whereon was inscribed, in large letters, and in all the freshness of newly sprung plants, the full name of

GEORGE WASHINGTON.

"THERE, Pa!" said George, quite in an ecstasy of astonishment, "did you ever see such a sight in all your life time?"

"WHY it seems like a curious affair, sure enough, George!"

"BUT, Pa, who did make it there, who did make it there?"

"It grew there by *chance,* I suppose, my son."

"By *chance,* Pa. O No! no! it never did grow there by *chance,* Pa; indeed that it never did!"

"HIGH! why not, my son?"

"WHY, Pa, did you ever see any body's name in a plant bed before?"

"WELL, but George, such a thing might happen, though you never saw it before."

"Yes, Pa, but I did never see the little plants grow up so as to make *one single* letter of my name before. Now, how could they grow up so as to make *all* the letters of my name! and then standing one after another, to spell *my name so exactly!*—and all so neat and even too, at top and bottom!! O Pa, you must not say *chance* did all this. Indeed *somebody* did it; and I dare say now, Pa, *you* did it just to scare *me*, because I am your little boy."

His father smiled, and said, "Well, George, you have guessed right—I indeed *did* it; but not to *scare* you, my son; but to learn you a great thing which I wish you to understand. I want, my son, to introduce you to your *true* Father."

"HIGH, Pa, an't you my *true* father, that has loved me, and been so good to me always?"

"YES, George. I am your father, as the world calls it: and I love you very dearly too. But yet with all my love for you, George, I am but a poor good-for-nothing sort of a father in comparison of one you have."

"AYE! I know, well enough whom you mean, Pa. You mean God Almighty, don't you?"

"YES, my son, I mean him indeed. *He is* your *true* Father, George."

"But, Pa, where is God Almighty? I did never *see* him yet."

"True, my son; but though you never *saw* him, yet he is always with you. You did not see me when ten days ago I made this little plant bed, where you see your name in such beautiful green letters; but though you did not *see* me here, yet you know I was here!!"

"Yes, Pa, that I do—I know you was here."

"WELL, then, and as my son could not believe that *chance* had made and put together so exactly the *letters* of his name, (though only sixteen) then how can he believe that *chance* could have made and put together all those millions and millions of things that are now so exactly fitted to his good! That my son may look at every thing around him, see! what fine eyes he has got! and a little pug nose to smell the sweet flowers! and pretty ears to hear sweet sounds! and a lovely mouth for his bread and butter! and O, the little ivory teeth to cut it for him! and the dear little tongue to prattle with his father! and precious little hands and fingers to hold his playthings! and beautiful little feet for him to run about upon! and when my little rogue of a son is tired with running about, then the still night comes for him to lie down, and his mother sings, and the little crickets chirp him to sleep! and as soon as he has slept enough, and jumps up fresh and strong as a little buck, then the sweet golden light is ready for him! When he looks down into the water, there he sees the beautiful silver fishes for him! and up in the *trees* there are the apples, and peaches, and *thousands* of sweet fruits for him! and *all, all around* him, wherever my dear boy looks, he sees everything just to his *wants* and *wishes;* the bubbling springs with cool sweet water for him to drink! and the wood to make him sparkling fires when he is cold! and beautiful horses for him to ride! and strong oxen to work for him! and the *good* cows to give him milk! and bees to make sweet honey for his sweeter mouth! and the little lambs, with snowy wool, for beautiful clothes for him! Now, these and all the *ten thousand thousand other good things* more than my son can ever think of, and all so exactly fitted to his *use* and *delight*—Now how could chance ever have done all this for my little son? Oh George!"

He would have gone on, but George, who had hung upon his father's words with looks and eyes of all-devouring attention, here broke out:

"OH, Pa, that's enough! that's enough! It can't be chance, in-deed, it can't be chance, that made and gave me all these things."

"WHAT was it then, do you think, my son?"

"INDEED, Pa, I don't know, unless it was *God Almighty!*"

"YES, George, he it was, my son, and nobody else."

"WELL, but Pa, (continued George) does God Almighty give me *everything?* Don't you give me *some things,* Pa?"

"I GIVE *you* something indeed! Oh how can I give you any thing, George! I who have nothing on earth that I can call my own, no, not even the breath I draw!"

"HIGH, Pa! isn't that great big house your house, and this garden and the horses yonder, and oxen, and sheep, and trees, and every thing, isn't all yours, Pa?"

"OH no! my son! no! why you make me shrink into nothing, George, when you talk of all these belonging to *me,* who can't even make a *grain of sand!* Oh, how could I, my son, have given life to those great oxen and horses, when I can't give life even to a fly! no! for if the poorest fly were killed, it is not your father, George, nor all the men in the world, that could ever make him alive again!"

At this, George fell into a profound silence, while his pensive looks showed that his youthful soul was laboring with some idea never felt before. Perhaps it was at this moment that the good Spirit of God ingrafted on his heart that germ of *piety,* which filled his after life with so many of the precious fruits of *morality.*

JOHN MARSHALL[2]

General Washington was rather above the common size, his frame was robust, and his constitution vigorous . . . capable of enduring great fatigue, and requiring a considerable degree of exercise for the preservation of his health. His exterior created in the beholder the idea of strength united with manly gracefulness.

His manners were rather reserved than free, though they partook nothing of that dryness and sternness which accompany reserve when carried to an extreme; and on all proper occasions, he could relax sufficiently to show how highly he was gratified by the charms of conversation, and the pleasures of society. His person and whole deportment exhibited an unaffected and indescribable dignity, unmingled with haughtiness, of which all who approached him were sensible; and the attachment of those who possessed his friendship and enjoyed his intimacy, was ardent but always respectful.

His temper was humane, benevolent, and conciliatory; but there was a quickness in his sensibility to any thing apparently offensive, which experience had taught him to watch and to correct.

In the management of his private affairs he exhibited an exact yet liberal economy. His funds were not prodigally wasted on capricious and ill-examined schemes, nor refused to beneficial though costly improvements. They remained therefore competent to that expensive establishment which his reputation, added to a hospitable temper, had in some measure imposed upon him; and to those donations which real distress has a right to claim from opulence.

He made no pretensions to that vivacity which fascinates, or to that wit which dazzles and frequently imposes on the understanding. More solid than brilliant, judgment rather than genius constituted the most prominent feature of his character.

As a military man, he was brave, enterprising, and cautious. That malignity which has sought to strip him of all the higher qualities of a general, has conceded to him personal courage, and a firmness of resolution which neither dangers nor difficulties could shake. But candor will allow him other great and valuable endowments. If his military course does not abound with splendid

[2] John Marshall, *The Life of George Washington* (Philadelphia, 1807), V, 773–79.

achievements, it exhibits a series of judicious measures adapted to circumstances, which probably saved his country.

Placed, without having studied the theory, or been taught in the school of experience, the practice of war, at the head of an undisciplined, ill-organized multitude which was unused to the restraints and unacquainted with the ordinary duties of a camp, without the aid of officers possessing those lights which the commander in chief was yet to acquire, it would have been a miracle indeed had his conduct been absolutely faultless. But, possessing an energetic and distinguishing mind, on which the lessons of experience were never lost, his errors, if he committed any, were quickly repaired; and those measures which the state of things rendered most advisable were seldom if ever neglected. Inferior to his adversary in the numbers, in the equipment, and in the discipline of his troops, it is evidence of real merit that no great and decisive advantages were ever obtained over him, and that the opportunity to strike an important blow never passed away unused. He has been termed the American Fabius; but those who compare his actions with his means will perceive at least as much of Marcellus as of Fabius in his character. He could not have been more enterprising without endangering the cause he defended, nor have put more to hazard without incurring justly the imputation of rashness. Not relying upon those chances which sometimes give a favorable issue to attempts apparently desperate, his conduct was regulated by calculations made upon the capacities of his army, and the real situation of his country. We called a second time to command the armies of the United States, a change of circumstances had taken place, and he meditated a corresponding change of conduct. In modelling the army of 1798, he sought for men distinguished for their boldness of execution, not less than for their prudence in counsel, and contemplated a system of continued attack. "The enemy," said the general in his private letters, "must never be permitted to gain foothold on our shores."

In his civil administration, as in his military career, were exhibited ample and repeated proofs of that practical good sense, of that sound judgment which is perhaps the most rare, and is certainly the most valuable quality of the human mind. Devoting himself to the duties of his station, and pursuing no object distinct from the public good, he was accustomed to contemplate at a distance those critical situations in which the United States might probably be placed; and to digest, before the occasion required action, the line of conduct which it would be proper to observe. Taught to distrust first impressions, he sought to acquire all the information which was attainable, and to hear, without prejudice, all the reasons which could be urged for or against a particular measure. His own judgment was suspended until it became necessary to determine, and his decisions, thus maturely made, were seldom if ever to be shaken. His conduct therefore was systematic, and the great objects of his administration were steadily pursued.

Respecting, as the first magistrate in a free government must ever do, the real and deliberate sentiments of the people, their gusts of passion passed over without ruffling the smooth surface of his mind. Trusting to the reflecting good sense of the nation for approbation and support, he had the magnanimity to pursue its real interests in opposition to its temporary prejudices; and, though far from being regardless of popular favor, he could never stoop to retain by deserving to lose it. In more instances than one, we find him committing his whole popularity to hazard, and pursuing steadily, in opposition to a torrent which would have overwhelmed a man of ordinary firmness, that course which has been dictated by a sense of duty.

In speculation, he was a real republican, devoted to the Constitution of his country, and to that system of equal political rights on which it is founded. But between a balanced republic and a democracy, the difference is like that between order and chaos. Real liberty, he thought, was to be preserved only by preserving the authority of the laws, and maintaining the energy of government. Scarcely did society present two characters which, in his opinion, less resembled each other than a patriot and a demagogue.

No man has ever appeared upon the theatre of public action whose integrity was more incorruptible, or whose principles were more perfectly free from the contamination of those selfish and unworthy passions which find their nourishment in the conflicts of party. Having no views which required concealment, his real and avowed motives were the same; and his whole correspondence does not furnish a single case from which even an enemy would infer that he was capable, under any circumstances, of stooping to the employment of duplicity. No truth can be uttered with more confidence than that his ends were always upright, and his means always pure. He exhibits the rare example of a politician to whom wiles were absolutely unknown, and whose professions to foreign governments and to his own countrymen were always sincere. In him was fully exemplified the real distinction which forever exists between wisdom and cunning, and the importance as well as truth of the maxim that "honesty is the best policy."

If Washington possessed ambition, that passion was, in his bosom, so regulated by principles, or controlled by circumstances, that it was neither vicious nor turbulent. Intrigue was never employed as the mean of its gratification, nor was personal aggrandizement its object. The various high and important stations to which he was called by the public voice were unsought by himself; and in consenting to fill them, he seems rather to have yielded to a general conviction that the interests of his country would be thereby promoted, than to his particular inclination.

Neither the extraordinary partiality of the American people, the extravagant praises which were bestowed upon him, nor the inveterate opposition and malignant calumnies which he experienced, had any visible influence upon his conduct. The cause is to be looked for in the texture of his mind.

In him, that innate and unassuming modesty which adulation would have offended, which the voluntary plaudits of millions could not betray into indiscretion, and which never obtruded upon others his claims to superior consideration, was happily blended with a high and correct sense of personal dignity, and with a just consciousness of that respect which is due to station. Without exertion, he could maintain the happy medium between that arrogance which wounds, and that facility which allows the office to be degraded in the person who fills it.

It is impossible to contemplate the great events which have occurred in the United States under the auspices of Washington, without ascribing them, in some measure, to him. If we ask the causes of the prosperous issue of a war, against the successful termination of which there were so many probabilities? of the good which was produced, and the ill which was avoided during an administration fated to contend with the strongest prejudices that a combination of circumstances and of passions could produce? of the constant favor of the great mass of his fellow citizens, and of the confidence which, to the last moment of his life, they reposed in him? The answer, so far as these causes may be found in his character, will furnish a lesson well meriting the attention of those who are candidates for political fame.

Endowed by nature with a sound judgment, and an accurate discriminating mind, he feared not that laborious attention which made him perfectly master of those subjects, in all their relations, on which he was to decide: and this essential quality was guided by an unvarying sense of moral right, which would tolerate the employment only of those means that would bear the most rigid examination; by a fairness of intention which neither sought nor required disguise; and by a purity of virtue which was not only untainted, but unsuspected.

FRANCOIS GUIZOT [3]

Washington had not those brilliant and extraordinary qualities which strike the imagination of men at the first glance. He did not belong to the class of men of vivid genius, who pant for an opportunity of display, are impelled by great thoughts or great passions, and diffuse around them the wealth of their own natures, before any outward occasion or necessity calls for its employment. Free from all internal restlessness and the promptings and pride of ambition, Washington did not seek opportunities to distinguish himself, and never aspired to the admiration of the world. This spirit so resolute, this heart so lofty, was profoundly calm and modest. Capable of rising to a level with the highest destiny, he might have lived in ignorance of his real power without suffering from it, and have found, in the cultivation of his estates, a satisfactory employment for those energetic faculties, which were to be proved equal to the task of commanding armies and founding a government. . . .

He had, in a remarkable degree, those two qualities which, in active life, make men capable of great things. He could confide strongly in his own views, and act resolutely in conformity with them, without fearing to assume the responsibility. It is always a weakness of conviction that leads to weakness of conduct; for man derives his motives from his own thoughts more than from any other source. From the moment that the [Revolutionary] quarrel began, Washington was convinced that the cause of his country

[3] Francois Guizot, *Essay on the Character and Influence of Washington in the Revolution of the United States of America* (Boston, 1840), pp. 59–61, 63–66, 120–21, 124–25.

was just, and that success must necessarily follow so just a cause, in
a country already so powerful. Nine years were to be spent in war
to obtain independence, and ten years in political discussion to
form a system of government. Obstacles, reverses, enmities, treachery, mistakes, public indifference, personal antipathies, all these
encumbered the progress of Washington during this long period.
But his faith and hope were never shaken for a moment. . . .

The same strength of conviction, the same fidelity to his own
judgment, which he manifested in his estimate of things generally,
attended him in his practical management of business. Possessing
a mind of admirable freedom, rather in virtue of the soundness of
its views, than of its fertility and variety, he never received his
opinions at second hand, nor adopted them from any prejudice;
but, on every occasion, he formed them himself, by the simple
observation or attentive study of facts, unswayed by any bias or
prepossession, always acquainting himself personally with the actual truth.

Thus, when he had examined, reflected, and made up his mind,
nothing disturbed him; he did not permit himself to be thrown
into, and kept in, a state of perpetual doubt and irresolution,
either by the opinion of others, or by love of applause, or by fear
of opposition. He trusted in God and in himself. . . . Whether
the occasion was of great or little moment, whether the consequences were near at hand or remote, Washington, when once
convinced, never hesitated to move onward upon the faith of his
conviction. One would have inferred from his firm and quiet
resolution that it was natural to him to act with decision and assume responsibility—a certain sign of a genius born to command;
an admirable power, when united to a conscientious disinterestedness. . . .

Washington's natural inclination was rather to a democratic social state than to any other. Of a mind just rather than expansive,
of a temper wise and calm; full of dignity, but free from all selfish and arrogant pretensions; coveting rather respect than power;
the impartiality of democratic principles, and the simplicity of
democratic manners, far from offending or annoying him, suited
his tastes and satisfied his judgment. He did not trouble himself
with inquiring, like the partisans of the aristocratic system,
whether more elaborate combinations, a division into ranks, privileges, and artificial barriers, were necessary to the preservation of
society. He lived tranquilly in the midst of an equal and sover-

eign people, finding its authority to be lawful and submitting to it without effort.

But when the question was one of political and not social order, when the discussion turned upon the organization of the government, he was strongly federal, opposed to local and popular pretensions, and the declared advocate of the unity and force of the central power. He placed himself under this standard, and did so in order to insure its triumph. But still his elevation was not the victory of a party, and awakened in no one either exultation or regret. In the eyes, not only of the public, but of his enemies, he was not included in any party and was above them all. . . .

A man of experience and a man of action, he had an admirable wisdom, and made no pretensions to systematic theories. He took no side beforehand; he made no show of the principles that were to govern him. Thus, there was nothing like a logical harshness in his conduct, no committal of self-love, no struggle of rival talent. When he obtained the victory, his success was not to his adversaries either a stake lost or a sweeping sentence of condemnation. It was not on the ground of the superiority of his own mind that he triumphed; but on the ground of the nature of things, and of the inevitable necessity that accompanied them. Still his success was not an event without a moral character, the simple result of skill, strength, or fortune. Uninfluenced by any theory, he had faith in truth, and adopted it as the guide of his conduct. He did not pursue the victory of one opinion against the partisans of another; neither did he act from interest in the event alone, or merely from success. He did nothing which he did not think to be reasonable and just; so that his conduct, which had no systematic character, that might be humbling to his adversaries, had still a moral character which commanded respect.

HENRY T. TUCKERMAN [4]

There were . . . in that thinly-peopled region over which impends the Blue Ridge, beside the healthful freedom of nature, positive social elements at work. The aristocratic sentiment had a more emphatic recognition there than in any other of the English Cisatlantic colonies; the distinctions of landed property and

---

[4] Henry T. Tuckerman, *Essays, Biographical and Critical* (Boston, 1857), pp. 7–8, 10–11, 21–22.

of gentle blood were deeply felt; the responsibility of a high caste, and of personal authority and influence over a subject race, kept alive chivalric pride and loyalty; and, with the duties of the agriculturist, the pleasures of the hunt and of the table, and the rites of an established and unlimited hospitality, was mingled in the thoughts and the conversation of the people that interest in political affairs whence arise public spirit and patriotic enthusiasm. Thus, while estates carelessly cultivated, the absence of many conveniences, the rarity of modern luxuries, the free and easy habits of men accustomed rather to oversee workers than to work themselves, the rough highways, the unsubstantial dwellings and sparse settlements, might not impress the casual observer as favorable to elegance and dignity, he soon discovered both among the families who boasted of a Cavalier ancestry and transmitted noble blood. The Virginia of Sir Walter Raleigh—a country where the most extravagant of his golden dreams were to be realized—had given place to a nursery of men, cultivators of the soil, and rangers of the woods, where free, genial, and brave character found scope. . . .

These advantages, however, Washington shared with many planters of the South, and manorial residents of the North, and they were chiefly negative. A broader range of experience and more direct influences were indispensable to refine the manners and to test the abilities of one destined to lead men in war, and to organize the scattered and discordant elements of a young republic. This experience circumstances soon provided. His intimacy with Lord Fairfax, who, in the wilds of Virginia, emulated the courteous splendor of baronial life in England, the missions upon which he was sent by the governor of the State, combining military, diplomatic, and surveying duties, and especially the acquaintance he gained with European tactics in the disastrous campaign of Braddock—all united to prepare him for the exigencies of his future career; so that, in early manhood, with the athletic frame of a hunter and surveyor, the ruddy health of an enterprising agriculturist, the vigilant observation of a sportsman and border soldier, familiar alike with Indian ambush, the pathless forest, freshets and fevers, he had acquired the tact of authority, the self-possession that peril alone can teach, the dignified manners of a man of society, the firm bearing of a soldier, aptitude for affairs, and cheerfulness in privation. To the keen sense of honor, the earnest fidelity, the modesty of soul, and the strength of purpose, which belonged to his nature, the life of the youth in his native home, the planter, the engineer, the ambassador, the representative, the gentleman, and the military leader, had thus added a harmony and a scope, which already, to discriminating observers, indicated his future genius for public life, and his competency to render the greatest national services. . . .

So intimately associated in our minds is the career of Washington with lofty and unsullied renown, that it is difficult to recall him as divested of the confidence which his fame insured. We are apt to forget that when he took command of the army his person was unfamiliar, and his character inadequately tested to the public sense. Officers who shared his counsels, comrades in the French war, neighbors at Mount Vernon, the leading men of his native state, and a few statesmen who had carefully informed themselves of his antecedent life and private reputation, did, indeed, well appreciate his integrity, valor, and self-respect; but to the majority who had enlisted in the imminent struggle, and the large number who cautiously watched its prospects before committing either their fortunes or their honor, the elected chief was a stranger. Nor had he that natural facility of adaptation, or those conciliating manners, which have made the fresh leader of troops an idol in a month, nor the diplomatic courtesy that wins political allies. If we may borrow a metaphor from natural philosophy, it was not by magnetism, so much as by gravitation, that his moral authority was established. There was nothing in him to dazzle, as in Napoleon, nothing to allure, as in Louis XIV, when they sought to inspire their armies with enthusiasm. The power of Washington as a guide, a chieftain, and a representative of his country, was based on a less dramatic and more permanent law; he gained the influence so essential to success—the ability to control others—by virtue of a sublime self-government. It was, in the last analysis, because personal interest, selfish ambition, safety, comfort—all that human instincts endear—were cheerfully sacrificed, because passions naturally strong were kept in abeyance by an energetic will, because disinterestedness was demonstrated as a normal fact of character, that gradually, but surely, and by a law as inevitable as that which holds a planet to its orbit, public faith was irrevocably attached to him. . . .

The world has yet to understand the intellectual efficiency derived from moral qualities—how the candor of an honest and the clearness of an unperverted mind attain results beyond the reach of mere intelligence and adroitness—how conscious integrity gives both insight and directness to mental operations, and elevation above the plane of selfish motives affords a more comprehensive, and therefore a more reliable view of affairs, than the keenest examination based exclusively on personal ability. It becomes apparent, when illustrated by a life and its results, that the cunning of a Talleyrand, the military genius of a Napoleon, the fascinating qualities of a Fox, and other similar endowments of statesmen and soldiers, are essentially limited and temporary in their influence; whereas a good average intellect, sublimated by self-forgetting intrepidity, allies itself forever to the central and permanent interests of humanity. The mind of Washington was eminently practical; his perceptive faculties were strongly developed; the sense of beauty and the power of expression, those endowments so large in the scholar and the poet, were the least active in his nature; but the observant powers whereby space is measured at a glance, and the physical qualities noted correctly—the reflective instincts through which just ideas of facts and circumstances are realized—the sentiment of order which regulates the most chaotic elements of duty and work, thus securing despatch and precision—the openness to right impressions characteristic of an intellect, over which the visionary tendencies of imagination cast no delusion, and whose chief affinity is for absolute truth—these noble and efficient qualities eminently distinguished his mental organization, and were exhibited as its normal traits from childhood to age. . . . By means of them he read character with extraordinary success. They led him to methodize his life and labors, to plan with wisdom and execute with judgment, to use the most appropriate terms in conversation and writing, to keep the most exact accounts, to seek useful information from every source, to weigh prudently and decide firmly, to measure his words and manner with singular adaptation to the company and the occasion, to keep tranquil within his own brain perplexities, doubts, projects, anxieties, cares, and hopes enough to bewilder the most capacious intellect and to sink the boldest heart.

WILLIAM E. WOODWARD [5]

One of the most significant facts about Washington's long

[5] William E. Woodward, *George Washington: The Image and the Man* (New York: Liveright Publishing Corporation, 1926), pp. 428–30. Copyright 1926 by Boni & Liveright. Reprinted by permission of the publisher.

and distinguished career is that he never formulated any coherent theory of government. Hamilton and Jefferson both worked out distinctly articulated systems of politics. Each stood for a definite, cogent set of ideas of social structure. But there is nothing in the body of American political thought that we can call Washingtonism.

At first impression his political character appears utterly nebulous. His writings are a vast Milky Way of hazy thoughts. We turn their thousands of pages, marking sentences and paragraphs here and there, hoping to assemble them and build up a substantial theory of the common weal.

Can it be that this huge aggregation of words has no impressive import? We are about to think so; however, when we study them in detail we find that his observations are sensible, sane and practical. Yet somehow, they do not coalesce; they lack a fundamental idea, a spirit that binds them all together.

That was our first conclusion, but then we were thinking in terms of the great philosophies . . . of Rousseau, of Locke, of Adam Smith, of Voltaire, or Ricardo. Later one day, we thought of the mind of the large city banker, and we saw Washington's political personality in a flash of revelation. Washington thought as almost any able banker who might find himself in the eighteenth century would think.

The banker stands for stability, and Washington was for that. The banker stands for law and order, for land and mortgages, for substantial assets—and Washington believed in them, too.

The banker wants the nation to be prosperous; by that he means that he wants poor people to have plenty of work and wealthy people to have plenty of profits. That was Washington's ideal.

The banker does not want the under-dog to come on top; not that he hates the under-dog, but he is convinced that people who have not accumulated money lack the brains to carry on large affairs, and he is afraid they will disturb values. The banker is not without human sympathy; but he is for property first, and humanity second. He is a well-wisher of mankind, though in a struggle between men and property, he sympathises with property.

In this we see Washington's mind. A coherent political philosophy is not an impelling necessity to this type of intellect. The banker-mind is for any political party which does not overturn the accepted axioms of valuation.

Washington's ideas of government were not broad nor lucid, but they were very substantial.

DOUGLAS S. FREEMAN [6]

Washington had deep and dedicated love of country, a patriotism that sprang, originally, from his belief that Americans were being denied their inherited, inalienable rights, the surrender of which without a struggle was unworthy of self-respecting men. Little by little, as the contest went on, in spite of difficulty, and as the concept of union slowly developed, he began to see that independence would establish a new empire. He had been too busy with the crowded foreground to survey the far horizon of this idea, but more and more of it was visible . . . over the mountains. Combativeness and ambition hardened the steel of Washington's patriotism. The more his country was endangered, the more firmly did he resolve to defend her to the last; the more nearly hopeless his task, the greater his ambition to discharge it. This was why he almost always had a rebound of optimism from the announcement of some catastrophe—the abandonment of Ticonderoga, the surrender of Charleston, or the defeat of Gates at Camden.

His courage and his firm will matched his patriotism. So manifest was his physical bravery and so often proved that not even his most venomous personal enemies, Charles Lee and Thomas Conway, ever dared call it in question. Washington had, in addition, courage of a much higher order, the courage to admit error, to assume responsibility and to help a hard-pressed comrade at risk to his own Army and his own prestige. Above all, he had the courage and the will to go straight on where the road was blackest.

Caution was a characteristic as marked as his courage, but it never was displayed in a manner to sap his fortitude or to give the least suggestion of cowardice to anything he did as a soldier or as an individual. When he hesitated to attack, it was because he feared the defeat of his Army might be the ruin of the American cause. Personally, his caution had roots that went to the very heart of the man. He did not wish to become involved in personal disputes or to make embarrassing connections. He was cautious, also, and deliberate, because he did not wish to take the risk of

[6] Douglas S. Freeman, *George Washington, A Biography* (New York: Charles Scribner's Sons, 1952), V, 488–501. Copyright 1952 by Charles Scribner's Sons. Reprinted by permission of the publisher.

doing injustice by hasty action. Even more frequently, he paused and pondered lest the course he followed or the counsel he offered Congress or colleague would bring blame on him and cost him the good opinion of his fellowmen.

Sound judgment seemed of the very nature of the man. He would listen to half a dozen proposals, would deliberate on them, and almost certainly would choose the best. It was the same with the interpretation of spies' reports; it was so in his choice of men for a particular task whenever a choice was open to him.

"Patience," he said, "is a noble virtue, and, when rightly exercised, does not fail of its reward." He exemplified his maxim and he scarcely ever lost patience except in dealing with three classes— cowards, those whom he believed to be of habitual rascality, and, above all, those who were cheating the American people for their own profit in the life-and-death struggle for independence.

He was as diligent and systematic as he was patient. The time required for a given task was closely calculated; allowance for contingencies always was made. Whether directing a battle or a day's affairs, he usually was calm and cheerful.

Another essential element of his character, apparent to everyone who made the test, was the inflexible justice which already has been described in its relation to his leadership. Washington had discovered that justice was as useful and prudential as it was right. Nothing so surely assuaged hurt feelings or turned the ambition of lieutenants into proper channels as their conviction that they would receive complete justice at his hands. If controversy did develop, he had advantage and a measure of self-confidence from the outset when he knew that he had been absolutely just.

Infused into every other prime attribute, and a marked virtue in itself was the unfailing regard Washington had for civil authority. Nothing offended him more than the suggestion of any sort of dictatorship. Ambition had always to yield to law. The object of war was peace. Every soldier had a supreme, compelling duty to respect the government that would guard his rights and his property when its independence had been won.

Most of these eight cardinal characteristics were the flowering or development of qualities Washington had shown, perhaps immaturely, by the end of the French and Indian War. Besides these, Washington had, of course, numerous lesser characteristics of which his officers had spoken with puzzlement, with surprise, or with admiration. Always, for example, he displayed good will to decent men, even though he might not be prepared to accept them forthwith as friends. His consideration was equally broad. Twice only during the Revolution was he accused of a lack of regard for the sensibilities of others and in that instance, when he was alleged to have neglected Massachusetts legislators, he humbly promised reformation, though he was unaware of how he had given offence. The other occasion was when he arrived an hour late at a Yorktown dinner and made no apology. Washington disliked personal clashes and sought to avoid them. If he thought he had shown temper in dealing with an individual, he went out of his way to be sure he atoned for it. His treatment of Alexander Hamilton after their unpleasantness on the stairs at headquarters was altogether characteristic of him. The General still had no spontaneous sense of humor and while he occasionally indulged a laugh, it was over a bit of horseplay or some ludicrous harmless accident. In this, he prized what he did not possess opulently. "It is assuredly better," he said, "to go laughing than crying through the rough journey of life."

He would have been surprised had he known that he himself probably was an object of occasional amusement to some of the officers by reason of the strange contrasts of character he unconsciously presented. Cautious as he was in war, he remained at heart the bold man of business, and when he went into upper New York State with George Clinton he displayed no less keen an interest in land bargains than in battlefields. Again, Washington admonished his nephew Bushrod against speculation. Possessed though he was of every type of the courage a man might covet, he had one fear, which he avowed frankly to himself, as, for instance, when he abandoned the effort to prevail on Barras to make Boston the base of the French fleet: he dreaded the blame that might be visited on him if disaster resulted from an insistence of his own military judgment. Public censure was his supreme fear.

Still again, he held to his own acquisitiveness and carried it at least to the limit of reasonable application when he submitted Martha's travel bills for settlement by Congress. At the same time, he continued to make expensive changes at Mount Vernon during the war, and in August, 1782, when his funds were so low that he had to draw the money against his expense account, he donated fifty guineas to the first college named after him. ". . . let your hand give in proportion to your purse" he told Bushrod, and, while admitting that "not every one who asketh . . . deserveth charity," he added earnestly, "all, however, are worthy of the inquiry, or the deserving may suffer." To this there was one proviso in his mind—that in his charities and his more intimate benefactions, there must be no cheating, no attempt to take advantage of him. If this occurred, it ended good will even though he might have reasons for continuing his gifts. This applied even in the strangest mystery of Washington's life, his lack of affection for his mother. His added years and understanding brought no improvement in his relations with her. As a matter of filial duty, he had left instructions with Lund before he quit Mount Vernon that his mother's calls for money were to be met, and he assumed that this had been done, but apparently he did not write her even once during the war. He who had so much magnanimity and patience in dealing with human frailty was still so much like his mother, in most money matters, that he felt she had been grasping and unreasonable.

A similar contrast existed in his nature between pity and grief. He always had pity. It inspired much of his charity and no little of his effort, though his pity often was mingled with wrath against those responsible for human misery. Grief was different. Doubtless it was personal to him but outwardly in his attitude to it he had not changed since his youthful days when the death of his benefactor, Col. William Fairfax, brought from his pen a tribute of one clause only. During the Revolutionary War, the deaths that came closest to him were those of Alex. Scammell and John Laurens. The sole reference to the loss of Scammell, former Adjutant General and one of the ablest of regimental officers, was a sentence in a dispatch to Congress, "I am sorry to inform you"—with a few words on the circumstances of the wounding and capture of the gallant Colonel. John Laurens had been one of the most valuable of aides, as diligent and versatile a man as the service boasted. The circumstances of his death were heart-breaking, because he was killed in resisting a petty foraging raid, when the country was awaiting the completion of the peace treaty. Washington mentioned the tragedy twice, and not more than twice in his correspondence. To Greene he wrote appreciatively of Laurens's service, but to Lafayette he said merely, "Poor Laurens is dead," and added less than twenty words on the details, without a syllable of praise. His comrades did not blame Washington for this. Perhaps they told themselves he hid his feelings lest a show of grief would be a discouragement.

These and similar contrasting minor characteristics of Washington were as plain to his discerning revolutionary associates as his major virtues were. Deeper in the soul of the man, there was a frontier where he set up a barrier of defence, probably because he still was not sure of his strength and weakness there, and also because the citadel of his soul lay close beyond that line. Here was the scene of more than one spiritual dispute, and here the battleground of his resentments. "Personal enmity I have none, to any man," he awkwardly wrote Rev. Jacob Duché, when the repentant former Chaplain of Congress sought to return to the United States. Washington had wrestled with himself to achieve that goal and he believed he had conquered his temper, but on occasion he still flared up. The reason will appear in its proper place; the reality was a partial loss of self-mastery without which he might become a partisan later in life.

To this same uncertain frontier of Washington's mind his personal religion had been brought back after the years of peace had led him, the vestryman and then the warden, to conform without heart searching to the practices of the church. He had believed that a God directed his path, but he had not been particularly ardent in his faith. The war had convinced him that a Providence had intervened to save America from ruin. So often had he remarked it that a French skeptic would have said of him, no doubt, that a fatalist had become superstitious. On the other hand, had a Chaplain at headquarters been privileged to look through Washington's files he would have been disappointed to find there no evidence of expressed personal belief in any creedal religion. It was almost as if the God of Battles had subordinated the God of the humble heart. The tone of Washington's addresses and circulars was distinctly more fervent, to be sure, than in 1775, if the theme touched religion, but this change had not became marked until Jonathan Trumbull, Jr., had joined the staff and had begun to write Washington's public papers of this type. Trumbull's alternate and successor in this capacity was David Humphreys, who, like the Connecticut Governor's son, was of theologically minded New England believers. The part these two men played in accentuating and enlarging with their pens the place that Providence had in the mind of Washington probably was among the most extraordinary and least considered influences of puritanism on the thought of the young nation. The people who heard the replies of Washington to their addresses doubtless thought they were listening to the General, as indeed they were, to the extent that Washington did not cancel what had been written; but the warmth of the faith was more definitely that of the aide than that of the Commander-in-Chief. Now that the war had ended and the Providence that Washington would observe was that of rain and sunshine and season and storm, not that of marches and battles, it remained for the returning soldier to see whether God again became personal to him.

Another uncertainty on this frontier of Washington's mind was the effect of the adulation he was receiving. As a young man his modesty had been listed with his amiability as one of his most attractive qualities. His distrust in 1775 of his qualifications for supreme field command may have originated in a cautious regard for the reputation he previously had acquired, rather than in his modesty, but the result was the same: it led his colleagues in Congress to believe that he did not "think more highly" of himself than he should. Within less than a year after that, he had been subjected to the praise of the grateful city of Boston, which expressed the wish that "future generations" might "raise the richest and most lasting monuments to the name of Washington."

He frankly had liked this. The addresses of the Bay State representatives, he confided to his brother, exhibited "a pleasing testimony of their approbation of my conduct and of their personal regard, which I have found in various other instances, and which, in retirement, will afford many comfortable reflections." Congress had voted a medal; all America had smiled in approval. Then, in the summer of 1776 began the grim succession of defeats and disappointments—Long Island, Kip's Bay, White Plains, Fort Washington, Fort Lee, the retreat across Jersey. These events certainly presented no temptation for Washington to exalt himself—and neither did they have the contrary effect. There was nothing self-deprecatory about him, then or thereafter. Until after the French alliance, his behavior had bespoken a belief that modest manners were an evidence of good taste proper for a gentleman. It was not so much that he manifestly was humble as it was that he did not want to appear arrogant. Later, the French soldiers, particularly some of those under Rochambeau, poured out a sort of praise for which Washington had not been prepared. His admiring allies called it compliment; the British would have stamped it flattery; but it showed Washington that he already had in Europe a measure of the approbation he had sought to win in America. When to this was added in 1783 the vote of an equestrian statue, the laudation of the continent, and receptions that had the spirit of triumphant entry, had they combined to turn Washington's head? If ultimate victory and the homage of the people had failed to move him, he would have been the strangest of mortals; and if he had felt no pride in the completion of his task, he would have depreciated the magnitude of what had been accomplished. He did have pride but, as will appear later, it was related to something deeper than mere performance. Outwardly, even though Alexander Hamilton accused him of self-love and Charles Lee, in effect, alleged that Washington destroyed every rival, there was at the end of the war no evidence in him of exalted self-esteem. If he showed any change, it was in a keener taste for the formal addresses presented him, a somewhat more frequent use of "I" when he wrote, and a measurable rise in self-confidence.

On the same borderland between the visible defences and the citadel of Washington's spirit was the shadow he cast, the image he created in the minds of men. Was he dramatic? Did he seek to inspire or to impress the troops by his appearance? He had more respect for his ego than for his abilities, and he drew a distinction between himself and his position. In personal dealings he continued to display amiable, courteous and simple dignity; officially he had been a symbol of discipline and authority. Always, too, he had taken pains, as man and as commander, not to do anything that would make him appear ridiculous. This sharp sense of the fitness of things kept him from being pompous and theatrical; but circumstance or a developed appreciation of the dramatic aspects of military life had served to overcome what might have seemed to be in 1775 a cold lack of imagination in command. He still was not theatrical and he showed no self-consciousness on great occasions, unless his manifest if momentary emotion might be so classified; but he now was able to express his feelings in a few fitting words or even in a gesture that moved spectators. Beyond this, who can say whether, for example, there was studied art in his manner when he took out his spectacles to read Joseph Jones's letter at the Newburgh meeting and remarked to his officers, as he did so, that he had grown gray in their service and now was growing blind. Could he have been acting deliberately the role of a departing hero when he embraced each of his comrades in the farewell at Fraunces' Tavern? He had begun, also, at 51 years of age to speak in patriarchal phrases when he answered addresses—

did this mean that he had come to regard himself as the Moses of America?

Perhaps some of Washington's lieutenants knew there were at least two interpretations of some of these characteristics. Friends might have analyzed them correctly, and might have explained his peculiarities along with his patriotism, his courage, his judgment, his patience, his systematic diligence, his sense of justice and his respect for civil authority. Knox or Jonathan Trumbull, Jr., or David Humphreys, or almost any other of those who remained with him to the end might have taken him apart, quality by quality, but they could not easily have put him back together again. They could have said that to a certain point he was an understandable personality, of normal, integrated abilities—and, so saying, none of these men would have explained Washington or his success. Later critics were to examine the springs and wheels and escapement of his character, in applying to him the metaphor of a clock that he himself used to describe the Army and the people, but these critics could not discover readily what made him "tick."

Failure to understand the inmost man was not the result of any obtuseness on the part of Washington's companions in arms. Not many of them had known him prior to 1775; few had any acquaintance with his development during the French and Indian War; not one senior officer was familiar at first hand with his boyhood ambitions. He was himself responsible, in part, for the fact that he was a stranger, in his inmost self, to those around him. As man and soldier, he had built up through the years of war two walls of reserve. One had a footing of personal caution. "It is easy to make acquaintances," he explained, "but very difficult to shake them off, however irksome and unprofitable they are found after we have once committed ourselves to them. . . ." The safe rule of personal relationship, as he saw it, was this: "Be courteous to all but intimate with few, and let those few be well tried before you give them your confidence; true friendship is a plant of slow growth. . . ." If, in a different metaphor, he held, perhaps deliberately, to the caution enjoined in Polonius's counsel to Laertes, he grappled with "hoops of steel" those men whose "adoption" he had "tried." They never had been numerous—George William Fairfax, William Fitzhugh, Burwell Bassett, his brothers—all of them friends of earlier years. During the war he had added to that number two or three of his aides and, above all, Lafayette. He loved the young Marquis as he might have loved a son, but even in this

closest of friendships, Washington did not admit Lafayette all
the way beyond the second wall of his reserve, the wall of military
secrecy. In this, Washington's caution must have amused the few
who heard that he went so far as to disregard orders from Congress in November 1778, to give Lafayette a copy of his remarks
on the invasion of Canada. His treatment of the subject, Washington told Congress, "opens such a prospect of our wants and our
weakness as, in point of policy, ought only to be known to ourselves." In the final test, Washington regarded even Lafayette as
not of "ourselves."

The Commander-in-Chief knew how ears were raised in camp to
catch the faintest whisper of impending movement, and he realized, also, that gossips were almost as dangerous as the spies who
apparently watched from every clump of trees. The reasoning usually was applied so resolutely by Washington that few ever were
able to look over this wall of military reserve or to whisper
proudly, "The General told me. . . ." The one indiscreet utterance
charged against him publicly, that of his criticism of Destouches's
expedition, tightened his lips and stayed his pen; but even this
embarrassment had not led him, at the close of the war, to wrap
himself in the cerements of silence. Before inquisitive strangers
and loosely talking comrades, he appeared in a tightly buttoned
uniform, so to say; when alone with trusted aides, he unbuttoned
his coat; only in occasional letters to his brothers or in conversation with a few tested friends did he allow himself the shirtsleeves
of candor. Even where he knew his remarks would not be passed
on, reserve on military matters gradually was becoming a habit,
though not as yet a fixed habit, of personal relations, also.

Another reason some of Washington's colleagues did not understand how he had achieved what seemed impossible in the revolution was the human disposition to assume that large results
have complicated causes. These men, and many of those who came
after, felt there must be some elaborate explanation of Washington's accomplishments and character. Although his words usually
were the mirror of his mind, and his nature was disclosed daily in
the transaction of business, none of his comrades in arms could believe he actually was as simple as he had proved himself to be in
the stripping ordeal of war. That long trial of spirit had shown
the value of the experience he had acquired in the contest between France and England and during the years when he patiently
had developed Mount Vernon; but in a strange manner, to a most

surprising degree, the explanation of the General of 1775–83 is to be found in the surveyor of 1745–53. Certain qualities that seemed mildly different in a young man, and of no special importance, proved to be the foundation-stones of his character as military leader.

Washington gave an old friend, years later, the basic explanation of the success of his revolutionary leadership when he said he "always had walked on a straight line." Early in life he had acquired a positive love of the right, and he had developed the will to do the right. There must have been derelictions, but when his fame had created curiosity concerning his youth, there did not emerge even one gossip to tell a tale of tryst with a housemaid behind a haystack, or of a plundering escapade with boys of the neighborhood. The universal testimony was that he had been a "good boy," however imaginative some of the stories of particular acts may have been. By the time he reached his middle 'teens, he perceived that right-doing was profitable as well as honorable. He had developed immense ambition, also, and firm self-discipline by the continued exercise of his will. For all these reasons, he held rigidly to "walk on a straight line." Item-by-item scrutiny of his cash book and ledger, which are the fullest financial record of any young American of his generation, does not disclose one entry that even hints of a liaison with a woman. He had gambled a little on horses and on cards, and he had fallen harmlessly in love with his neighbor's wife, but out of this, and out of all his adventures at frontier posts, there developed no scandal. He wrote in 1799 "as far as human frailties and perhaps strong passions, would enable him," he had endeavored to "discharge the relative duties to his Maker and fellow men." If the "frailties" were serious, he overcame them, and he conquered the passions. He entered the Revolution with a genuine integrity of spirit, a possession of which he consciously was proud, though he did not boast of it. In his heart of hearts, he knew that no enemy could bring up against him truthfully any charge of misconduct that would hamper him in the discharge of his duty or discredit him in the eyes of honest men and women. In an unusual sense of the words, he "feared no evil," though he remained consistently cautious.

The next essential fact was his complete dedication of himself to the duties assigned him in 1775. He had told Congress the day he accepted command, "I will enter upon the momentous duty and exert every power I possess in their service for the support of the glorious cause." In that resolution, he had fought "with a halter round his neck." For months on end, he thought the next post might bring news that all his possessions on the Potomac had been destroyed. The most for which he had hoped in event of defeat, was that he would find an asylum on the Ohio. Neither this prospect nor any of a thousand disappointments had shaken his resolution.

Because Washington knew he had integrity and absolute dedication to the cause of independence, he had throughout the Revolution a positive peace of mind. This did not mean that he observed without concern the miseries of his men or the desperate fluctuation of American fortunes. Over these things he agonized endlessly; but always he could war the better against Britain because he was not at war with himself. None of his energies had to be diverted from administration and planning and operations in order to combat selfish ambition or to overcome distracting passions. His will and his long self-discipline were his rod and his staff.

As much a part of the man as integrity, dedication and peace with himself were the two rewards Washington desired for himself. He wanted first the assurance that he had kept his promise to devote himself completely to his task. It was *de profundis* that he had written Lund Washington, amid the miseries of Morristown: "You ask how I am to be rewarded for all this? There is one reward that nothing can deprive me of, and that is the consciousness of having done my duty with the strictest rectitude, and most scrupulous exactness, that if we should, ultimately, fail in the present contest, it is not owing to the want of exertion in me. . . ."

The other reward sought by Washington represented in developed form his youthful craving for what he had termed "honor." The "greatest of earthly rewards," he said, was "the approbation and affections of a free people." Other men might want ships or mistresses, or race horses and luck at cards; his ambition was that of deserving, winning and retaining the goodwill of right-minded Americans. If that ambition were considered a vanity, he would regret a verdict that was itself in some degree a forfeiture of good opinion, but as he had been from youth, so he was now in full manhood. Although he had no "favorite verse" of Holy Writ, the one that completely stated his ambition was the familiar proverb, "A good name is rather to be chosen than great riches"; and if at the end of the Revolutionary War he had to be characterized in a single sentence, it would be substantially this: He was a patriot of conscious integrity and unassailable conduct who had given himself completely to the revolutionary cause and desired for himself the satisfaction of having done his utmost and of having won the approval of those whose esteem he put above every other reward.

If his officers had seen clearly what Washington in reality was and what he sought, they would have realized how perfectly his cardinal virtues, his lesser characteristics and even some of his peculiarities fitted into the pattern of his life. His patriotism was absolute because it represented a supreme ideal to which he had resolved to be loyal at any price. His moral courage was high because he neither had failed to offer America his honest best, nor had done anything of which to be ashamed. Cheer was merely an expression of this courage. He was just because justice was right and because lack of it would cost him some of his self-respect. He could not be fair to himself if he were unjust to others. Courtesy and consideration had similar foundations. When faith wavered, he mustered composure in the knowledge that any display of concern by him would alarm and might demoralize his officers. In most tests of judgment, of temper and of patience, his long self-discipline served him so adequately that it was like the balance of a trained skater, so nearly automatic that it never seemed to involve effort. No honorable measure of self-restraint was too great a price to pay for the satisfaction of living up to his ideal of complete dedication to his trust; but when it came to public approbation, there was one price he would not pay: he would not purchase popularity by impairing his moral capital.

Washington's conscious integrity and resulting absence of war with himself gave him a certain self-confidence at the same time that they framed most of his resentments. If he justly were accused of error he would acknowledge it and would seek amendment; but if the charge were one that implied deliberate neglect of duty or any act that did not square with his knowledge of his integrity, he would fight back on the instant. Off the field of battle, almost every display of temper by Washington during the war had its origin in his belief that his integrity was being assailed. In a different way, a mind deliberately kept free of personal enmity was better able to reach sound conclusions. Good judgment fashioned the rounds on the ladder of Washington's ambition. Still again, his patience, one of his stoutest qualities, was built of will and self-discipline, but it had among its components his faith in America's future, his knowledge that time was slow, and his reconciliation to the fact that the men

capable of unselfish leadership were few in number. All these contributions to Washington's patience were, in turn, the expression
of his caution and of his integrity.

To explain one mystery is not to create another. In accepting the
integrity, the dedication and the ambitions of Washington as reali-
ties, one does not face an insoluble problem when one asks how this
life, at the end of the Revolution, had reached the goal of service,
satisfaction and reward. George Washington was neither an American Parsifal nor a biological "sport." What he was, he made himself
by will, by effort, by discipline, by ambition and by perseverance.
For the long and dangerous journeys of his incredible life, he had
the needful strength and direction because he walked that "straight
line."

"Straight line" . . . The Psalmist had chosen slightly different
words in giving the same answer to the old, old question: "Where-
withal shall the young man cleanse his way? By taking heed there-
to. . . ."

J. A. CARROLL [7]

Of the several presidents of the United States who have
served their countrymen memorably in critical periods, none experienced so full a measure of public esteem in the hour of inau-
guration as George Washington. No chief executive has entered
office better known to his contemporaries. From New England to
Georgia in 1789 Washington was celebrated as the American At-
las, the American Fabius, the Cincinnatus of the Western Hem-
isphere; for almost a decade now he had heard references to
himself as "Father of his Country." In 1783, upon retirement to
his farm after eight years as Commander in Chief of the Continental Army, he was by all odds the most famous man in America. Even as proprietor of Mount Vernon he had been conspicuous, a kind of national host whose beautiful home on the Potomac
became, as he said, a "well-resorted tavern" for unexpected and
unannounced travelers of every type. His appearance at the Philadelphia Convention in 1787 brought him again into public view,
and the architects and advertisers of the Constitution were quick
to dramatize the fact that General Washington had presided at

[7] J. A. Carroll, "George Washington," in Morton Borden, ed., *America's Ten
Greatest Presidents* (Chicago: Rand McNally & Company, 1961), pp. 6–11. Reprinted by permission of the publisher.

the rebuilding of the old Articles of Confederation into the "New Roof of Federalism." So familiar was his name by 1788 that no other could be mentioned seriously for the highest office in the new system of government. James Madison, major draftsman of the Constitution, visited Mount Vernon often and brought all his logic to bear against Washington's reluctance to leave retirement. From New York Alexander Hamilton sent urgent notes: "I take it for granted, Sir, you have concluded to comply with . . . the general call of your country in relation to the new government. You will permit me to say, that it is indispensable you should lend yourself to the first operation." The General still hesitated. "At my age and in my circumstance," he wrote, ". . . I have no wish which aspires beyond the humble and happy lot of living and dying a private citizen on my own farm." But his preference did not decide the matter. "We cannot, Sir, do without you," wrote Thomas Johnson of Maryland, adding that "thousands more" were in agreement. The first presidential election was a formality in the strictest sense, and unanimity was inevitable. The soldier-farmer from Virginia was the one American that his fellow-citizens, be they Federalists or "anti-Feds," knew best of all.

It is curious, then, that perhaps no president has proven more mysterious to posterity than the first. Historians have found it reasonably easy to chronicle the events of Washington's two administrations because the records and literary remains of the years 1789–97 are abundant. They have been able to dissect and to understand the opposite philosophies, social and economic, of the dominant personalities of the period, Alexander Hamilton and Thomas Jefferson. In detailed monographs they have shown how the clashing concepts of these two men ignited a political fire which, despite Washington's avowed determination to "walk on a straight line" and to act as "President of all the people," quickly divided the nation into sectional parties—Federalists following Hamilton northward and eastward, Republican-Democrats following Jefferson southward and westward. Scholars have identified party strife in the United States with the revolutionary upheavals that convulsed Europe in the 1790's, and possibly some have gone too far in ascribing "Anglomania" to Federalist leaders and "Gallomania" to Republicans. Washington's administrations, in any case, have been much discussed by modern historians. Their specialized studies fill a long shelf, and their conclusions are distilled accurately in many textbooks. Yet, to Americans in the twentieth century, President Washington presents something of an enigma. Confident as we may be that we understand the period, we do not always understand the man.

For all the research and exposition and synthesis that scholars have lavished on the eight formative years that George Washington occupied the chair of state, the figure of the first president is remarkably vague. The American whom his contemporaries felt they knew so well in 1789 has become increasingly a puzzle to subsequent generations. Gilbert Stuart's "Landsdowne" portrait, representing Washington in presidential costume of black velvet, will always be familiar, but its subject does not stand today in clear relief. Vapors of obscurity surround Washington in his role as chief executive. While many historians have been careful to point out and to praise the qualities of statesmanship that he possessed in depth, still a vagueness persists. Still the question was heard: What kind of president, really, was George Washington? . . .

Like a good poem, George Washington's character is perhaps better sensed than analyzed. It is better, in any case, to contemplate Washington in full size than to examine him by synthetic lens. Washington was not an architect in ideas; he was essentially a man of deeds. His thoughts do not array themselves in a convenient constellation that may be understood in outline; rather they form a massive milky way that must be considered from end to end. Washington does not emerge spontaneously in a pattern; he appears gradually in a procession of events. He is best portrayed not in composite overview, but by scrutiny of his thoughts and interpretation of his actions at climactic moments of his career. The cumulative method does not produce an image rapidly, but it has its delights. Douglas Southall Freeman, who studied Washington in this way for almost ten years while writing a large biography, regarded it an inestimable privilege to "live" so long in the company of a magnificent man. Others will find every hour they spend with Washington to be equally rewarding.

Reduced to enumeration, the achievements of Washington's administrations count to not less than ten. During his presidency the United States government gained its executive and legislative precedents, appended a bill of rights to the Constitution, established its credit at home and abroad, fostered manufacturing and encouraged commerce, survived a serious insurrection in the mountains of Pennsylvania, secured the transmontane frontier against

Indian depredations, effected the removal of British troops from the Old Northwest, checked Spanish encroachments in the Old Southwest and obtained transit rights on the Mississippi, forged a policy for the disposition of public lands, and avoided involvement in the vortex of European wars. Analysis will reveal that Washington's hand was large in many of these accomplishments, and that in several his role was decisive. Proud of their record, Federalists were quick to acknowledge this: Washington's leadership was never nebulous to them. "Such a Chief Magistrate," said Fisher Ames, "appears like the pole star in a clear sky. . . . His Presidency will form an epoch and be distinguished as the Age of Washington." Ames was an orator who arranged his words nicely, but he was also as intuitive and straight-speaking a Federalist as there was in the party. However reluctantly, Republicans came to the same conclusion. In 1796 Jefferson expressed it simply: "One man outweighs them all in influence over the people."

Yet, by the eyes of posterity, Washington's role has not been seen in so sharp a light. It has long been a fashion to regard President Washington's administrations not so much his as Alexander Hamilton's. Critical research in the twentieth century has established beyond question that the genius and energy of Hamilton were responsible for much that the Federal government did—and, indeed, for much of what happened in the United States—between 1789 and 1797. As Senator William Maclay, dour Republican of Pennsylvania, remarked testily, "Mr. Hamilton is all powerful and fails in nothing he attempts." No student of the period would deny Hamilton's significance, but it may be that emphasis on the brilliance of the "Young Lothario" of the Federalists has worked to the disadvantage of a deeper consideration of the President's own part in the affairs of the new republic. In its business, great and small, the President was always there. He was neither listless nor dull, as sometimes he has been portrayed, and neither too old nor too deaf to participate fully. "He was an Aegis," Hamilton admitted, "very essential to me."

Surely it is not incorrect to think of the Federalist era as the heyday of Hamiltonian ideals. But it is quite wrong to suppose that Washington loved the pomp and ceremony with which his aides surrounded him, that his attitudes were more English than American, or that he concurred readily with Hamilton's extreme and often-quoted remark on the necessity of rule by the "rich and wellborn." And it is altogether wrong to imagine that the President responded automatically to Hamilton's every suggestion, that he permitted a Svengali-like control to be exercised over him, or that he turned to Hamilton in helpless frustration when the pressures of office became too great.

Washington did none of these things. Instead, as chief executive, he developed to a remarkable degree the science of deliberate and responsible consultation. While Hamilton served as secretary of the treasury and Jefferson as secretary of state, Washington solicited advice from them almost equally. In 1789 and 1790 he consulted the "heads of departments" individually on specific matters, and made his decision largely on one officer's specific advice. By the end of 1791, however, he was calling them together for discussion of larger problems. The Cabinet met several times in 1792, and many times during Washington's second term. Washington's closest friend in the Cabinet was neither Hamilton nor Jefferson but rather his old military comrade, General Henry Knox, the secretary of war. It may be argued reasonably that Knox, who served until 1795, was a convenient mirror for Hamilton's views; but in these same years the President's thinking over a wide range of major problems more nearly approximated that of Edmund Randolph than of any other member of the Cabinet. This gifted Virginian was in no way a Hamiltonian Federalist—and, according to Jefferson, not very much of a Republican. Jefferson thought Randolph "indecisive" and a "chameleon." Washington thought him impartial and sound.

Randolph, one of the forgotten figures in American history, was Washington's protégé as a boy, then a Richmond lawyer and governor of Virginia, the first attorney general in 1789, and successor to Jefferson in the Department of State four years later. The President's faith in the judgment of Randolph was high, perhaps higher than historians have yet discovered, and the estrangement of the two men in 1795 amounted to a tragedy for each. For Randolph, who was accused of soliciting a French bribe and of defalcation in diplomatic funds, it meant disgrace and oblivion. For Washington, it meant the end of a treasured relationship. Only at this point, after the exit of the last member of his original Cabinet, did Hamilton's correspondence with Washington begin to reflect with startling vividity in the decisions of the President—and by now he was in the final year of his second term. No attempt is being made in these remarks to minimize the contributions of Hamilton to the policies and projects of Washington's government. They are meant only to underscore the central fact that, in the achievements of the Federalists between 1789 and 1797, the man who was President played a personal, an integral, and a most important part. . . .

R. ERNEST DUPUY AND TREVOR N. DUPUY [8]

Few Americans accept the legend of George Washington and the cherry tree. Yet most of us, including normally reputable historians and military analysts, seem still to think of Washington in terms which that legend represents. He is visualized as a man of awesomely noble rectitude, somewhat colorless in personal characteristics, tremendously impressive physically; a man of great courage and determination, but lacking real military genius. His ultimate victory is attributed to the fact that by personifying the nobility of the Revolutionary cause, and by his steadfast and unwavering devotion to that cause, he became the locus around which the patriots rallied, year after year, despite the many defeats he suffered at British hands, until French military assistance and British war-weariness finally forced King George to abandon the struggle.

There is, of course, some basis to this stereotype. There can be no doubt of the nobility of character of this austere man. He was defeated by the British on several occasions, and the ultimate victory was primarily due to his determination and steadfastness in the face of defeat and discouragement, plus the tremendous assistance rendered by the French. What is wrong with the stereotype, however, is its failure to recognize that defeat would have been inevitable if Washington had not been both a brilliant strategist and an extremely competent, charismatic battlefield leader. He did not ride to victory on the fighting and administrative capabilities of better soldiers—as has been suggested by admirers of such men as Greene, Steuben, Lafayette, Wayne, Morgan, de Grasse and Rochambeau—and even Benedict Arnold. He was not saved from disaster by ineptitude or lack of determination on the part of such opponents as the Howe brothers, Clinton, Cornwallis or Burgoyne. Washington both shaped and exploited the successes of his most able subordinates. The top British leadership in the Revolution was relatively competent in terms of eighteenth-century warfare;

---

[8] R. Ernest Dupuy and Trevor N. Dupuy, *The Compact History of the Revolutionary War* (New York: Hawthorn Books, Inc., 1963), pp. 474–75. Reprinted by permission of the publisher.

if these men made more mistakes than Washington, and if he was able to take advantage of their mistakes, this should redound to his military credit, rather than providing a mere excuse for victory.

It is our opinion—substantiated, we believe, by the facts presented in our text—that Washington was by far the most able military leader, strategically and tactically, on either side in the Revolution. He started the war in 1775 as an inexperienced commander, well aware of his own deficiencies. By 1781 he had developed a competence worthy of favorable comparison beside Alexander at the Granicus, Caesar at the Rubicon, Hannibal at the Alps, Genghis Khan at the Great Wall, Frederick the Great at Prague, or Napoleon at Montenotte. In other words, if he had been called upon to fight further after Yorktown, it is our contention that Washington would have merited inclusion in the very limited ranks of the great captains of history.

THOMAS A. BAILEY [9]

If we must rank Presidents, Washington, in my judgment, deserves the place at the very top. He not only passes most of the standard tests with flying colors, but in several significant respects is in a class by himself.

First, the Constitutional Convention, over which Washington had presided, specifically tailored the presidency to fit him, in the hope and expectation that he would accept the high office. The resulting Constitution, which was narrowly ratified anyhow, probably would have lost out if the people had not been assured that their beloved general would serve. He could be trusted not to subvert their liberties with these vast new powers, because he had spurned a suggested kingship and had gladly laid down quasi-dictatorial authority when the War of Independence ended.

Second, Washington was the one truly "indispensable man." With his towering prestige, unfaltering leadership, and sterling character, he was the only figure able to command the confidence necessary to get the new ship of state off on even keel. He was perhaps the only man in the history of the presidency bigger than

[9] Thomas A. Bailey, *Presidential Greatness* (New York: Meredith Press, 1966), pp. 267–69. Copyright 1966 by Thomas A. Bailey. Reprinted by permission of the publisher.

the government itself. Hamilton, Jefferson, and Madison all urged him to serve; and Hamilton and Jefferson, in agreement on little else, insisted that he subject himself to a second term. Even Vice President Adams, though eaten with envy and in line for the office himself, privately conceded that Washington had to be drafted again. The Republic was not yet sufficiently united to fall in step behind a New England sectionalist like Adams.

Third, the absence-of-blunders test leaves Washington with a uniquely high mark. Although his every move could be deemed a potential precedent binding generations unborn, his foot did not slip once. He made no major mistakes—something that cannot be said of any of his successors who served long enough to make a mistake. The Irish-British historian W. E. H. Lecky, writing of Washington's leadership during the Revolution, concluded that "of all the great men in history," the august Virginian was the most "invariably judicious." Perhaps his only real failure, at least administratively, was his failure to mix fire and water, that is, to persuade Hamilton and Jefferson to work together harmoniously in his cabinet.

Washington has been criticized for having been too aristocratic, too monarchical, too friendly to legislation favoring the wealthy bigwigs. But statesmen must be judged in the context of their times, and the monarchical, aristocratic past was too recent to permit a clean break. Even if Washington had been disposed to do so, which he was not, he could not have ushered in Jacksonian democracy or even Jeffersonian democracy. He admittedly "packed" the federal offices with conservative-minded Federalists who were favorable to the Constitution. He would have been criminally derelict in his duty if he had done less. The Constitution was going to get off to a wobbly enough start at best, and it almost certainly would have been scuttled if entrusted to the hands of its enemies. As for the charge that Washington used undue force in crushing the Whiskey Rebellion in Pennsylvania, he was determined to establish the authority of the new government once and for all, and that he did.

If, as Henry Lee's eulogy proclaimed in 1799, Washington was "first in war, first in peace, and first in the hearts of his countrymen," in more ways than one he was first among the Presidents. I have no quarrel with the experts who put him in the Great category, only I would place him ahead of Lincoln in the premier position.

JAMES T. FLEXNER [10]

An intelligent comparison between Washington and the celebrated soldiers of the past is greatly impeded by a fact too often
overlooked: Washington was never truly a military man. He remained to the end of the war a civilian serving half-reluctantly in
uniform. If we read Washington's writings beside those of any
dedicated warrior . . . it is instantly clear how little the basic bent
of his mind was military. The numerous metaphors he wrote down
in armed camps are almost never drawn from warfare: they recall
the fields and forests, the mounting and sinking suns of a peaceful
home. He never wrote of a Revolutionary battle in terms of san-
guinary exultation; he never, in all his exhortations to his troops,
appealed to bloodlust or glorified carnage. Such happy visions of
military adventure as he had enjoyed as a younger man and in an
earlier war had faded from him. "It is time," he admonished Chas-
tellus, "for the age of knight-errantry and mad heroism to be at an
end." The French staff officer Barbé-Marbois wrote, "I have been
told that he preserves in battle the character of humanity which
makes him so dear to his soldiers in camp."

Washington would take military risks to protect what he referred
to as "the essential interests of any individual." He wrote, "The
misfortunes of war, and the unhappy circumstances frequently at-
tendant thereon to individuals, are more to be lamented than
avoided: but it is the duty of everyone to alleviate these as much as
possible." Although recognizing the military genius of Harry Lee,
he was horrified by the cruelties that dedicated soldier perpetrated.
Congressman Charles Carroll of Carrollton complained of Washington, "He is so humane and delicate that I fear the common cause
will suffer. . . . The man cannot be too much admired and lamented."

While the true military mind is most concerned with the exertion of force, Washington considered force secondary in winning the
war to gentleness, justice, forbearance. This was because the unre-
constructed civilian was, as he stated again and again, infinitely less
afraid of military defeat than of doubt and disunity within the
patriot cause.

[10] James T. Flexner, *George Washington in the American Revolution* (Boston: Little, Brown and Company, 1968), pp. 531–32, 538–40. Copyright ©
1967 by James T. Flexner. Reprinted by permission of the publisher.

Although he never abandoned the hope of a sledgehammer blow that would end the war overnight, from week to week and year to year such a quick solution remained a seductive will-o'-the-wisp. In the long reaches, Washington used the army as a propaganda instrument. "Popular expectations," he wrote, "should always be complied with where injury in the execution is not too apparent, especially in such a contest as the one we are engaged in, where the spirit and willingness of the people must in a great measure take the place of coercion."

. . . As Washington's self-education carried him ever further away from accepted military ideas, he turned from imported books and his original advisers to discussions with new men whom he had personally guided through the same school of experience where he himself still studied. One reason for the successes of the French Revolutionary armies was that, the old hierarchical officer corps having been shattered, naturally brilliant soldiers were able to rise to leadership apart from birth, wealth, and precedent. The same was true in Washington's army. Of the leading generals who opened the war, none except Washington remained till the end influential. Indeed, only Gates and Washington were still in active service.

Washington encouraged to rise around him Arnold, a disreputable apothecary and trader who (before he turned traitor) became the greatest combat general of the war; Knox, the overweight bookseller who taught himself the fine art of artillery; Greene, the ironmonger with a stiff knee whom those who deny the honor to Washington consider the conflict's ablest all-round general; Lafayette, the twenty-year-old spoiled darling of the French Court who, for all his wildly romantic and egotistical talk, became a cautiously effective general; Hamilton, another twenty-year-old, this one a bastard from the Indies, in whom Washington found the ideal staff officer; the brilliant John Laurens, who might, had it not been for his untimely death, have been one of the greatest of the younger Founding Fathers. Of Washington's final inner team only Steuben had come to the army with accepted military knowledge, and the bogus baron was in European terms a fraud: his contribution was to make drill over again, under American advice, in a manner that suited the American army.

When Washington went increasingly his own way, he was plagued by his former dependences. Reed and Mifflin could not believe that the man whose early palpitations they had witnessed could ever become a brilliant commander. Gates and Lee became convinced that Washington had fallen into the hands of incompetent sycophants, all the more because, after consulting with new men, he was heretical to his old advisers' teachings. The idea that Washington was sinking into military ineptitude was further encouraged by high-ranking European volunteers, men like Conway who had come from abroad as convinced as were the British regulars that they were bringing with them the ultimate answers. All this contributed, during 1777 and 1778, to fracases. Washington, the usually mild, struck out with his gigantic limbs, and the older order went down. Since the new order remained on the whole loyal to the man who had created and trained them, Washington became, in his control of the American military, unrivaled. This unique position contributed, in itself, toward the eventual victory.

Afterword

The process of mythology whereby Washington was converted from fallible human to faultless saint began early and was exceedingly rapid and thorough. Even while Americans still mourned his death, an itinerant book peddler and evangelist, Mason Locke Weems, decided to enrich himself (financially) and the nation (morally) by penning a series of mainly spurious anecdotes revealing the "Great Virtues" of Washington. The work of this clever charlatan, which first appeared in 1800, had an enormous impact, probably greater than that of any single volume in American history. It satisfied the public yearning to venerate Washington, to hear homilies of his life, accounts of his piety and patriotism, his wisdom and dedication, above all, his incorruptibility. Other heroes might possess blemishes, but Washington, as "Father of his country," needed to appear spotless. Thus he was presented by Weems and his countless imitators; thus he was envisioned by Americans. Abraham Lincoln owned the tenth edition and learned its lessons well. "To add brightness to the sun or glory to the name of Washington is alike impossible," he proclaimed on February 22, 1842. "Let none attempt it. In solemn awe pronounce the name, and in its naked deathless splendor leave it shining on."

Of course there were always a few who resisted the unqualified acclaim. Ralph Waldo Emerson remarked that people bored with such unstinting praise were apt to remark in private, "Damn George Washington!" One of William M. Thackeray's characters in the play *The Virginians* shouts: "Hang him! He has no faults and that's why I dislike him." Artemus Ward poked fun at the image: "G. Washington was abowt the best man this world ever sot eyes on. . . . He never slopt over!"

By canonizing Washington the people placed him in a class separate from all other heroes. Everyone—the most recent immigrant, the youngest schoolchild, the ignorant and illiterate—could identify Washington. But they could not identify with him. Partly the celestial image was at fault. "It might be set apart for individual homage," according to one observer, yet "the mass of a nation could neither conceive nor appreciate it." Washington may have been "first in war" and "first in peace" but it is questionable whether he was "first in the hearts of his countrymen." Americans could not love him as they did Benjamin Franklin, and later, Abraham Lincoln. He was too perfect, too dignified, too reticent, too humorless, and too patrician for a people who made a fetish of egalitarian democracy. Franklin they remembered with warmth for munching a roll while strolling the streets of Philadelphia; or Lincoln regaling his cabinet with a funny story. These two had the common touch Washington lacked. The truly great men of America, wrote William Dean Howells, "are notable for their likeness to their fellow-men, and not for their unlikeness." Using this index, Franklin ranked high, according to Howells, for his commonness prevented him from assuming "any superiority of bearing, and the unconscious hauteur which comes of aristocratic breeding."

If Washington was too aristocratic for liberals, he appeared to be too unsystematic for conservatives. The former elevated Jefferson as their favorite philosopher, and the latter placed Hamilton in that role. What some Federalists whispered, later scholars repeated: Hamilton was the true voice and spirit of the Washington administration. The history of the early nation was—and still largely is—viewed almost entirely as a conflict between their respective positions. Nor have writers been able to escape identification with either Jefferson or Hamilton. ("Alas," writes Merrill D. Peterson, "It is inescapable.") The same problem does not exist for Washington. He has been shunted aside.

By the twentieth century, then, Americans have alternately revered Washington, debunked him, and ignored him, but never have been able to know him. Only in the past few decades have scholars tried to peer behind the nineteenth-century curtain to discover the true Washington, to break the polarized interpretations and restore a proper balance to early national history, to attempt to separate the man and the myth. Perhaps the task is impossible. The name and figure of Washington are indelibly stamped upon the land. The capital of the nation; one state; hundreds of cities, towns, counties, and post offices; mountains, rivers and lakes; colleges, and even people are named after him. His face has been carved upon a mountain in South Dakota, and printed on the money and postage stamps which citizens use daily. In the capital a monument towers 555 feet, and numberless statues and portraits of Washington adorn parks and offices all across America. Annually, on February 22, a national holiday commemorates his birth. Perhaps the image is too strong for the man, and the two shall ever remain mixed, remote, mysterious, celestial, impregnable.

This much is certain: never has his legacy been more neglected, and even repudiated, than at present. Washington is too rational for an age which has made a cult of the irrational; he is too much the heroic figure for an age which celebrates the anti-hero. The virtues and values for which he was once honored are under attack —one hopes temporarily. Law and order, which Washington regarded as vital to the effective operation of democracy, is equated with repressive governmental controls. The moderation he preached and the practicality he endorsed are both rejected by young radicals and visionaries using the tactics of fear and violence. The patriotism he more than any other man symbolized is currently identified with nationalism and militarism. God is dead, some contemporaries declare, and so is the relevance of Washington.

On the chance they may be mistaken, the meaning of Washington should be repeated and punctuated. In 1799 he wrote that throughout his life he had "always walked a straight line, and endeavored as far as human frailties, and perhaps strong passions, would enable him, to discharge the relative duties to his Maker and fellow men, without seeking any indirect or lefthanded attempts to acquire popularity." His legacy was his character: motivated by love of country, guided by the wish to secure the liberty and happiness of the people, he assumed the grave responsibilities of leading America through the ordeals of war and the pangs of political formation. Throughout his character remained, as Thomas Jefferson said, "in its mass, perfect, in nothing bad, in few points indifferent; and it may truly be said, that never did nature and fortune combine more perfectly to make a man great." So long as America endures, Washington's character will remain a rod by which the performance of others are measured.

Bibliographical Note

Nineteenth-century collections of Washington's writings should be used with caution. Jared Sparks, the earliest and one of the most eminent editors, *Life and Writings of George Washington* (Boston, 1837–39), 2 volumes, omitted or even changed the text whenever Washington's words seemed to him offensive or crude. Thus a genial reference to "Old Put" becomes "General Putnam," and "rascally crews" becomes "the crews." Fortunately there is a first rate edition in 39 volumes for the student, John C. Fitzpatrick's *The Writings of George Washington* (Washington, D. C., 1931–44). There are several good one-volume samplers of Washington's writings, one of the most recent by Saul K. Padover, *The Washington Papers* (New York, 1955).

Equally to be avoided are the adulatory biographers of the nineteenth century and the debunking biographies of the 1920's. Both, of course, tell the reader more about the author and the time of composition than of the subject. For the former, the pattern was set by Mason Weems's book, the tenth edition of which was called *The Life of George Washington; with Curious Anecdotes, Equally Honorable to Himself and Exemplary to His Young Countrymen* (Philadelphia, 1810). Or one might look at a volume of even grander invention by Morrison Heady, *The Farmer Boy, and How He Became Commander in Chief* (Boston, 1864). For the latter, a typical effort is by William E. Woodward, *George Washington: The Image and the Man* (New York, 1926). Contemporary historians are fascinated as much by the growth of the Washington legend as by the man. Students interested in both are directed to Part Seven ("Search for Symbols") of Daniel J. Boorstin, *The Americans: The National Experience* (New York, 1965); Bernard Mayo, *Myths and Men* (Athens, Georgia, 1959); J. A. Carroll, "George Washington," in Morton Borden, ed., *America's Ten Greatest Presidents* (Chicago, 1961); and the splendid book by Marcus Cunliffe, *George Washington: Man and Monument* (Boston, 1958).

Washington Irving's *Life of George Washington* (New York, 1855–59), 5 volumes, is completely a narrative account, with little or no interpretation. Woodrow Wilson's *George Washington* (New York, 1896) is an undistinguished effort. There are some valuable insights in the accounts of Washington written by Chateaubriand, Guizot, and Tuckerman. But one does not get a sense of balance until the work of Rupert Hughes, *George Washington* (New York, 1926–30), 3 volumes.

The finest multivolume biographical study is by Douglas Southall

Freeman, *George Washington: A Biography* (New York, 1948–57), 7 volumes (the final volume by J. A. Carroll and Mary W. Ashworth). Freeman keeps the focus on the central figure. All events are viewed through Washington's eyes, all issues debated and resolved as Washington considered them. What emerges, then, is not only an excellent treatment of the times, but of the character of its major figure. This is biography at its best. For dissenting opinion, however, see Walter Hendrickson, "A Review of Reviews of Douglas S. Freeman's *Young Washington*," *Library Quarterly*, XXI (July, 1951), 173–82.

Recent and superior one-volume studies are by Francis Bellamy, *The Private Life of George Washington* (New York, 1951), and Esmond Wright, *Washington and the American Revolution* (London, 1957). For Washington and foreign affairs, see Alexander DeConde, *Entangling Alliance: Politics and Diplomacy under George Washington* (Durham, 1958). For Washington's military ability, a new astute account by James T. Flexner, *George Washington in the American Revolution* (Boston, 1968), is highly recommended. For Washington as President the reader is urged to compare the treatments in Joseph Charles, *The Origins of the American Party System* (Williamsburg, 1956), and John C. Miller, *The Federalist Era, 1789–1801* (New York, 1960).

Index